Maths

11+ Handbook

OXFORD

UNIVERSITY PRESS

Contents

Introduction

Number

Fractions and decimals

Handling data

Shape and space

Measurement

Everyday practice

Introduction

What is an 11+ Maths exam?

A maths test is a common test for the 11+ exam and although the content is rooted in the National Curriculum at Key Stage 2, the depth and breadth of questions asked might be more challenging for some children. This may be especially so with children who lack confidence in the subject.

The 11+ exam is taken by children at the end of Year 5 or in Year 6. It is a test used by state-funded grammar schools, selected academies and many independent schools. It is used to select the children who perform the best under exam conditions, and to place them in a school environment with peers of a similar academic ability. Unlike most other exams, selective entrance tests cannot usually be retaken (although some schools do still set exams for entry at 12+ or 13+), so there is often fierce competition to perform well and achieve good results.

There are two main exam boards involved in producing 11+ Maths exams: GL Assessment and CEM (Durham University). GL Assessment uses a separate paper for maths, while CEM tends to mix other 11+ subjects such as English, verbal and non-verbal reasoning with maths to create a paper divided into sections. There are other exam boards and individual schools who write their own papers and some schools will have the 11+ exam completed on a computer rather than on paper.

An 11+ Maths paper can be written in two formats, following either a multiple-choice or standard layout. For a multiple-choice paper, children will need to choose their answer from a set of options and mark it on a separate answer sheet. Answers must be marked in these booklets very carefully as the answer sheets are often read and marked by a computerised system. In the standard format, children must write each answer directly onto the question paper.

As with most exams, 11+ exam papers are timed, typically lasting between 45 minutes and one hour. The introduction of a time-limit can potentially have an impact on a child's performance, so it is important for children to work through practice materials in both timed and non-timed environments.

The scope and content of an 11+ Maths test can often differ across UK regions, as there is a range of question types that can be included. However, a paper will generally be testing a child's ability to:

- think and calculate quickly
- apply logical thinking and problem solving
- apply their knowledge of times tables

- apply the four number operations (+ − × ÷) accurately
- understand number relationships, measurement, geometry and data handling
- use mental arithmetic
- work systematically.

These skills are tested through a series of questions that include:

Numbers

This is to test the ability to understand place value, the decimal system, rounding numbers and using the four main operations, including long multiplication and long division techniques. Questions might cover factors, multiples, problem solving, sequences and algebra.

Fractions and decimals

This is to test the ability to understand fractions of numbers, mixed numbers, improper fractions, equivalent fractions and decimal fractions. Questions might include adding, subtracting, dividing and multiplying fractions, percentages, ratio and proportion.

Handling data

This is to test the ability to organise and compare information using a variety of charts, grids, graphs, Venn diagrams and timetables. Questions might include mean, median, mode and range and probability.

Shape and space

This is to test the ability to understand 2D and 3D shapes, angles, bearings, area, perimeter, volume and capacity. Questions might include triangle facts, quadrilateral and polygon facts and transformations (coordinates, reflection, rotation and translation, symmetry).

Measurement

This is to test the ability to understand metric and imperial units of measurement, reading scales, time and timetables. Questions might include time and date facts, map scales, and problem-solving using length, mass, volume and capacity.

This book will help you to understand the key questions found in 11+ Maths exams. The Bond range of maths assessment papers and the CEM maths and non-verbal reasoning books can be used alongside this book. The Bond series also provides a range of exam test papers in both multiple-choice and standard format that will provide exam-style practice papers.

Number

① *Place value*

Knowing the value of digits

You need to know the value of a digit wherever it appears in a number.

Multiplying and dividing by 10s, 100s and 1000s

TM	M	HTh	TTh	Th	H	T	O	•	t	h	th
tens of millions	millions	hundreds of thousands	tens of thousands	thousands	hundreds	tens	ones	decimal point	tenths	hundredths	thousandths
10 000 000	1 000 000	100 000	10 000	1 000	100	10	1		0.1	0.01	0.001

$\times 10$ $\div 10$

$\times 100$ $\div 100$

$\times 1000$ $\div 1000$

> **REMEMBER!**
>
> In this book, whenever a new maths word is introduced, it is printed in red. If you need to, you can check its meaning in the Glossary at the back of the book.

> **REMEMBER!**
>
> The 'ones' column is sometimes called the 'units' column.

When a whole number is **multiplied** by:

- **10**, all digits move **one** column to the **left**. If the ones column is empty a zero needs to be written in it.
- **100**, all digits move **two** columns to the **left**. If the ones or tens columns are empty, zeros need to be written in them.
- **1000**, all digits move **three** columns to the **left**. If the ones, tens or hundreds columns are empty, zeros need to be written in them.

When a number is **divided** by:

- **10**, all digits move **one** column to the **right**.
- **100**, all digits move **two** columns to the **right**.
- **1000**, all digits move **three** columns to the **right**.

"What about decimal numbers?"

As with **whole numbers**, when you use decimal numbers all digits in the number have to move in one direction and the same number of columns. Just remember to keep the digits in the same order!

$$147.5 \div 100 = 1.475$$

"What about numbers with no decimal point?"

Whole numbers can be written with a decimal point but must have one or more zeros in the columns representing tenths, hundredths, and so on:

$$73 = 73.0 = 73.0000000 \ldots$$

Rounding numbers

Rounding a number to the **nearest 10** means finding the nearest multiple **of 10**. Rounding a number to the nearest 100, 1000, 10 000 means finding the nearest multiple of 100, 1000, 10 000 to that number. You can round up or round down. Rounding up means finding the next largest multiple of your rounding number. Rounding down means finding the next smallest multiple of your rounding number. So, if you are rounding to the nearest 10, you go up or down to the next multiple of 10.

Look at this example:

Round **12 194** to the nearest **100**.

12 194

The digit in the **tens** column is **greater than five** so round **up** to the next multiple of 100. 194 is closer to 200 than 100.

12 194 rounded to the nearest 100 is **12 200**.

REMEMBER!

Look at the number in the column to the **right** of the one you are asked to round to. If it is **less than five**, round down. If it is **five or greater than five**, round up.

The same idea works for decimals, so you can round off to a certain number of decimal places. To decide whether you must round up or down, look at the digit to the right of the decimal place to which you need to round.

For example:

12.264 rounded to **one** decimal place (the nearest tenth) is **12.3**.

12.264 rounded to **two** decimal places (the nearest hundredth) is **12.26**.

Key facts

- The digits to the left of the decimal point show the number of ones, tens, hundreds and thousands, and so on. The digits to the right of the decimal point show the number of tenths, hundredths, thousandths, and so on.

- To **multiply** by 10, 100 or 1000, imagine the digits are written in the place-value columns and move them to the **left** to make the number larger.

- To **divide** by 10, 100 or 1000, move the digits to the **right** to make the number smaller.

- If the digit in the column to the **right** of the one you are asked to round to is **less than five**, round down. If it is **five or greater than five**, round up.

② *Addition and subtraction problems*

"I never know whether I'm supposed to be adding or subtracting."

Addition

An easy way to identify problems that can be solved using addition is to look out for these words, phrases and symbols – they all mean 'add':

> + how many altogether find the sum
>
> plus add increase find the total

Adding a whole number onto another number gives an answer **larger** than the number you started with.

To add on in your head, it can be helpful to start with the larger number and add on the smaller number or numbers in easy jumps.

Remember the jumps as you go and then add the jumps together.

> **REMEMBER!**
>
> When adding, look for pairs of numbers that add up to a multiple of 10:
>
> $4 + 18 + 6 = 10 + 18 = 28$
>
> $19 + 23 + 17 = 40 + 19 = 59$
>
> $479 + 243 + 511 = 990 + 243 = 1233$

It can be helpful to write the numbers one under the other to ensure you add together the digits in their columns.

For example:

```
    1 3 2 2
    2 4 8 3
  + 5 2 1 9
  ─────────
    8 0 0 0    Total the thousands
      9 0 0    Total the hundreds
      1 1 0    Total the tens
        1 4    Total the ones
  ─────────
    9 0 2 4    The grand total!
  ─────────
```

Subtraction

An easy way to identify problems that can be solved using subtraction is to look out for these words, phrases and symbols – they all mean 'subtract':

- –   subtract   minus   decrease
  find the difference   deduct   reduce   take away

Subtracting a positive number from another number gives an answer **smaller** than the number you started with. Usually at 11+ stage you subtract the smaller number from the larger number.

To subtract in your head, it can be helpful to start from the smaller number and count up to the larger number in easy jumps. Remember the jumps as you go and then add the jumps together.

Finding the difference between two numbers means the smaller number must be subtracted from the larger number. Alternatively you can count on from the smaller number to the larger number:

Find the difference between 843 and 387.

843 − 387

$$443 + 13 = 456$$

The difference between 843 and 387 is 456.

Addition and subtraction involving money

Rounding up to the next pound can make calculations involving money much easier to work out in your head. For example:

99p is nearly £1   £1.99 is nearly £2   £7.99 is nearly £8

But, remember to adjust your answer to deal with the penny difference!

Key facts

- The **opposite** or inverse of addition is subtraction.
- The **opposite** or inverse of subtraction is addition.
- **Add** is the same as **find the total, plus, increase, find the sum, how many altogether.**
- **Subtract** is the same as **take away, minus, find the difference, find the change, decrease, reduce, deduct.**
- Estimate answers (make a **sensible guess**) before you work out the actual answer.

Exam tips

In an exam, there may be limited space to write working out, so it is critical that you work neatly, systematically and carefully. Use your fingers, quick drawings or whatever you need to find the correct answer as quickly as possible.

③ *Multiplication and division problems*

"I'm never sure whether to multiply or to divide."

Multiplication

An easy way to identify problems that can be solved using multiplication is to look out for these words, phrases and symbols – they all mean 'multiply':

> ×   **multiply   times   find the product of**

Multiplying a number by a positive integer (whole number) gives an answer **larger** than the number you started with.

A multiplication grid can be drawn quickly and helps to break down difficult multiplication questions such as 326 × 42.

1 Set the multiplication up as a grid.

```
      3   2   6
×         4   2
    _____
```

2 Begin with 2 in the 'ones' or 'units' column:

$6 \times 2 = 12$ so we write the 2 in the ones column and carry over the 1 to the tens column. (Write it in small writing above the multiplication.)

Next we multiply 2×2 and add on the 1 we have carried over. This equals 5, so we write the 5 in the tens column.

Finally we have $3 \times 2 = 6$ so we write the 6 in the hundreds column.

```
          1
      3   2   6
×         4   2
    _____
      6   5   2
```

Number

11

3 Now we must multiply by the 4 in the tens column, so we are really multiplying by 40.

As 40 = 4 × 10, we can insert the 0 in the ones column and then multiply by 4 which is the same as multiplying by 40.

```
    1   2   1
        3   2   6
    ×       4   2
        6   5   2
1   3   0   4   0
```

So we calculate 6 × 4 = 24 and we write the 4 in the **tens** column and carry over the 2 and write it above the hundreds column.

Now we work out 2 × 4 and add on the 2 we have carried over. This equals 10, so we write the 0 in the hundreds column and carry over the 1 and write it above the thousands column.

Finally, we work out 3 × 4 and add on the 1 we have carried over. This equals 13 so we write the 13.

4 To complete our multiplication, we add up the two rows of the two parts of the multiplication.

```
    1   2   1
        3   2   6
    ×       4   2
        6   5   2
1   3   0   4   0
1   3   6   9   2
```

326 × 42 = 13 692

Division

An easy way to identify problems that can be solved using division is to look out for these words, phrases and symbols – they all mean 'divide':

÷) ‾‾‾‾   share   split into equal amounts   /
how many ... in ...   find the fraction...

Dividing a number by a positive integer (whole number) gives an answer **smaller** than the number you started with.

A number is divisible by a smaller number if the smaller number divides **exactly** into the larger number. So, 25 is divisible by 5 because 5 divides into 25 exactly.

This list of quick ways to test the divisibility of a number is very useful to learn.

A number is divisible by or a multiple of:

- 2 if it is even
- 3 if the sum of the digits is divisible by 3
- 4 if the last two digits are a number divisible by 4
- 5 if the ones digit is 5 or 0
- 6 if the number is even and divisible by 3
- 9 if the sum of the digits is divisible by 9
- 10 if the ones digit is 0

(See topic 5: Factors and multiples, page 16, to learn about multiples.)

You can **divide** by using **repeated subtraction**. This means taking the same amount away again and again until there is nothing left, or the remainder is smaller than the number you are subtracting. Your answer is the number of times you were able to subtract the amount, with the remainder if there is one.

REMEMBER!

The remainder is sometimes very important. For example, you might need to work out how many coaches are needed to take children on a school trip. If there are children remaining after coaches have been completely filled, then an extra coach will still be needed to take them on their trip!

Look at this example:

> **How many pencils costing 30p each can be bought for £8?**
>
> 1 Set up the 'bus stop method' and change £8 to 800p so we are dividing using the same units of measurement.
>
> $$30 \overline{)8 \quad 0 \quad 0}$$
>
> 2 How many 30s fit into 8? None, because 8 is smaller than 30, so we place a '0' above the 8 and look at 80.
>
> $$30 \overline{)\overset{0}{8} \quad 0 \quad 0}$$
>
> 3 How many 30s fit into 80? We know $2 \times 30 = 60$ so we write '2' above the first '0' and we place 60 underneath the 80 and subtract.
>
> $$30 \overline{) \begin{array}{ccc} \overset{0}{8} & \overset{2}{0} & 0 \\ 6 & 0 & \\ \hline 2 & 0 & \end{array}}$$
>
> 4 We 'bring down' the last '0' to give us 200.
>
> $$30 \overline{) \begin{array}{ccc} \overset{0}{8} & \overset{2}{0} & 0 \\ 6 & 0 & \downarrow \\ \hline 2 & 0 & 0 \end{array}}$$
>
> 5 How many 30s fit into 200? We know $6 \times 30 = 180$ so we write '6' above the final '0' and we place 180 underneath the 200 and subtract.
>
> $$30 \overline{) \begin{array}{ccc} \overset{0}{8} & \overset{2}{0} & \overset{6}{0} \\ 6 & 0 & \downarrow \\ \hline 2 & 0 & 0 \\ 1 & 8 & 0 \\ \hline & 2 & 0 \end{array}}$$
>
> 6 The remainder is 20p, not enough money to buy another pencil, so our final answer is 26 pencils. 26 pencils costing 30p each can be bought for £8.00 with 20p left over. The remainder (20p) is not enough to buy another pencil.

Key facts

- The opposite or **inverse** of multiplication is division.
- The opposite or **inverse** of division is multiplication.
- Multiply is the same as **find the product, times, groups** or **lots of.**
- Divide is the same as **share** or **split into equal amounts, partition** or **find a fraction.** You can say "**How many ... in ...?**" to help your thinking.
- A number is **divisible by** a smaller number if the smaller number divides **exactly** into the larger number, with no remainder.
- The answer in a division calculation is the **quotient.**

④ *Mixed or several-step problems*

"I never know what to do first with problems."

REMEMBER!

Really IMAGINE what is going on in a problem. If it helps, draw pictures or imagine yourself as the person mentioned in the problem, if there is one.

Problem-solving steps

Problems are often made up of many stages and you will need several different operations in order to find the answers. Following a clear set of steps, such as the '6-point plan' below, could make problems easier to work out.

1. Read the problem carefully; **think**: "What am I being asked to work out?"

2. Decide what you have to work out and which **number operation** you need. Write the calculation down.

3. Continue deciding what you must work out at **each step** and which number operation you need. Write the calculations.

4. Estimate the answer.

5. Work out the **answers** to the calculations in order.

6. Ask yourself: "Is my answer **reasonable** compared with my estimate?"

- There are four number operations: +, −, × and ÷. Look again at topics 2 and 3 to remind yourself of the different mathematical words used to mean add, subtract, multiply and divide.
- Try following the 6-point plan to help decide what you are being asked to do in a several-step problem.
- **Profit** means how much extra money you can earn if you sell something for more than it cost.

⑤ *Factors and multiples*

Factors

An easy way to be sure of finding all the factors in a number is to find them in pairs like this:

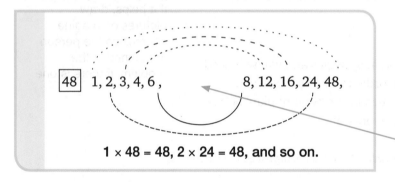

1 × 48 = 48, 2 × 24 = 48, and so on.

REMEMBER!

A **factor** is a whole number that will **divide exactly** into another number.

You know you have found all the factors when there are no possible factors between the middle two numbers.

You may have to find the highest common factor (HCF) of a set of numbers. To do this, find all the factors of the numbers you are given and see which factors they have in common or share. The largest one is the highest common factor.

Look at this example:

Find the HCF of 24, 42 and 48.
The factors of 24 are: 1, 2, 3, 4, **6**, 8, 12, 24.
The factors of 42 are: 1, 2, 3, **6**, 7, 14, 21, 42.
The factors of 48 are: 1, 2, 3, 4, **6**, 8, 12, 16, 24, 48.
The HCF of 24, 42 and 48 is **6**.

REMEMBER!

Prime factors are factors which are also prime numbers.

(To remind yourself about prime numbers turn to page 19.)

Multiples

A **multiple** of a number is the answer when it is multiplied by another number.

REMEMBER!

Remember that you have to **multiply** to get a **multiple**.

$4 \times 5 = 20$ 20 is a multiple of 4 and 5.

The multiples of 5 are 5, 10, 15, 20, 25, and so on.

You may have to find the lowest common multiple (LCM) of a set of numbers. To do this, write down the first few multiples of all the numbers. (Start with the highest number.) Check to see if one of these is a multiple of all the numbers. If not, try a few more until you find the LCM.

Look at this example:

> Find the LCM of 4, 6 and 9.
> The first five multiples of 9: 9, 18, 27, **36**, 45
> The first nine multiples of 4: 4, 8, 12, 16, 20, 24, 28, 32, **36**
> The first six multiples of 6: 6, 12, 18, 24, 30, **36**
> The LCM of 4, 6 and 9 is 36.

Key facts

- A **factor** is a whole number that will **divide exactly** into another number.

- The **HCF** (highest common factor) of a set of numbers is the largest number that is a factor of all numbers in the set.

- The **prime factors** of a number are the prime numbers which can be multiplied together to make that number.

- A **multiple** of a number is the answer when the number is multiplied by another number.

- The **LCM** (lowest common multiple) of a set of numbers is the smallest number that is a multiple of all numbers in the set.

⑥ Special numbers

There are some particular types of numbers that you need to be able to recognise. A short section on each of the eight main types is given on the next pages.

Negative numbers

On a number line positive numbers are to the right of 0 and are greater than 0. Negative numbers are to the left of 0 and are less than 0:

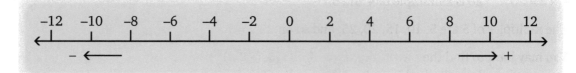

A thermometer shows positive and negative numbers on a vertical scale. Freezing point is zero degrees Celsius (0°C). Above zero are the positive numbers (getting warmer). Below zero are the negative numbers (getting colder).

Square numbers

The first twelve square numbers are:

1, 4, 9, 16, 25, 36, 49, 64, 81, 100, 121, 144.

4^2 means 'four **squared**', or four times four. The number in little writing (the index number) tells you that you must multiply **4** by itself.

$1 \times 1 = 1^2 = 1$

$2 \times 2 = 2^2 = 4$

$3 \times 3 = 3^2 = 9$

$4 \times 4 = 4^2 = 16...$

> **REMEMBER!**
>
> A **square number** is a number multiplied by itself.

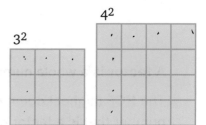

Cube numbers

The first six cube numbers are: **1, 8, 27, 64, 125, 216.**

4^3 means 'four **cubed**', or four times four times four. The index number tells you that you must multiply **4** by itself then multiply the answer by **4**.

$1 \times 1 \times 1 = 1^3 = 1$

$2 \times 2 \times 2 = 2^3 = 8$

$3 \times 3 \times 3 = 3^3 = 27$

$4 \times 4 \times 4 = 4^3 = 64...$

> **REMEMBER!**
>
> A **cube number** is a number multiplied by itself and by itself again.

   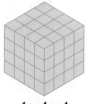

$1 \times 1 \times 1$ $2 \times 2 \times 2$ $3 \times 3 \times 3$ $4 \times 4 \times 4$

When a cube is built using centimetre cubes, starting with just one cube for the first cube, the number of cubes used to make the increasingly large cubes is the same as the cubed numbers.

Consecutive numbers

Consecutive numbers are numbers that follow on in order. So numbers such as **45, 46, 47, 48, 49, 50** are consecutive.

The numbers in a group like **46, 45, 47, 50, 49** are not consecutive.

REMEMBER!

Consecutive means 'in a row', or 'following in order'.

Prime numbers

The first 10 **prime numbers** are all less than 30:

2, 3, 5, 7, 11, 13, 17, 19, 23, 29

1 is not a prime number because it has only one factor: 1

2 is the only even prime number! Can you see why?

REMEMBER!

A **prime number** has only two factors: one and the number itself.

Roman numerals

Here are seven Roman numerals and their standard number values:

Roman	I	V	X	L	C	D	M
Standard	1	5	10	50	100	500	1000

You can make up any other whole number by using a combination of these seven Roman numerals. For example:

REMEMBER!

Dates and Kings/ Queens are sometimes written using Roman numerals:
MMXV = 2015
Henry VIII

IV = 4 (one less than 5)   VI = 6 (one more than 5)   IX = 9 (one less than 10)

XIII = 13 (10 + 3)   DXI = 511 (500 + 10 + 1)   CM = 900 (100 less than 1000)

You may also need to know the value of these Roman numerals:

XL = 40   LX = 60   XC = 90

Triangular numbers

If you arrange dots in a triangular pattern, then the increasing number of dots needed to make a triangle form the sequence of triangular numbers.

These are the first 10 triangular numbers:

1, 3, 6, 10, 15, 21, 28, 36, 45, 55

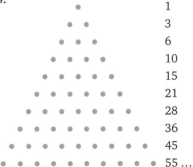

1
3
6
10
15
21
28
36
45
55 ...

Number

The difference between each pair of numbers goes up by 1 each time. The first difference is 2, then 3, then 4, and so on.

Square root

The square root of a number is the number you multiply by itself to make that number.

The square root of 100 is 10 because 10 × 10 is 100.

The square root of 49 is 7 because 7 × 7 is 49.

The symbol for a square root is: $\sqrt{\ }$. So, 'the square root of 49' is written as $\sqrt{49}$.

Key facts

- **Negative numbers** are less than zero: –1, –2, –3 … –74, … –201, …
- **Square numbers** are the result of multiplying a number by itself: 1 × 1, 2 × 2, … 6 × 6, …
- **Cube numbers** are the result of multiplying a number by itself and by itself again: 1 × 1 × 1, 2 × 2 × 2, … 6 × 6 × 6, …
- **Consecutive numbers** follow on in order: 21, 22, 23.
- **Prime numbers** have only two factors (1 and the number itself): 2, 3, 5, 7, …
- **Roman numerals:** letters represent numbers, for example: V = 5, X = 10, L = 50, C = 100, D = 500, M = 1000. (See page 19 for more examples.)
- **Triangular numbers start at 1, then add 2, then add 3**, and so on: 1, 3, 6, 10, 15, …
- **A square root** is the number you multiply by itself to make a larger number.

(7) Sequences

Common number patterns

Maths is largely about seeing patterns. You need to know and be able to recognise some of the most common and useful patterns. Here are some sequences and patterns you should already know.

Multiples: e.g.	7, 14, 21, 28...
Prime numbers:	2, 3, 5, 7...
Odd numbers:	1, 3, 5, 7...
Triangular numbers:	1, 3, 6, 10...
Even numbers:	2, 4, 6, 8 ...
Doubling numbers: e.g.	1, 2, 4, 8 ...
Square numbers:	1, 4, 9, 16 ...
Halving numbers: e.g.	64, 32, 16, 8 ...
Cube numbers:	1, 8, 27, 64 ...

Finding the rule

To find the missing number in a sequence, first find out the rule. It can be very helpful to write the difference between each pair òf numbers along the sequence to help you find the rule.

Some sequences will go up or down by the same number each step. Others may go up or down one more or less than the previous step.

Be careful: some patterns go alternately in pairs or even in threes! So, if you can't find a pattern between pairs of numbers and the numbers aren't in size order, then check to see if there are two or three sequences in one.

For example, write the next two numbers in this sequence:

First, write the difference between each pair of numbers:

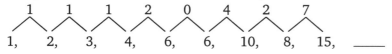

There doesn't appear to be a pattern so try looking at every other number (alternate numbers):

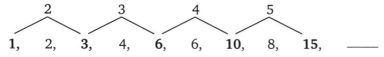

These are triangular numbers. The next number would be 21 (add 6).

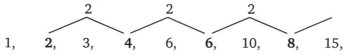

These are even numbers. The next number would be 10.

The next two numbers in the sequence are 10, 21.

⑧ *Equations and algebra*

Equations

An **equation** is a number sentence where one thing is **equal** to something else. An equals sign, =, shows that the numbers to the left of it must be equal to, or have the same value as, the numbers to the right.

Look at this equation: 3 + 4 = 7

Three plus four is equal to seven. Both sides of the equation are balanced. They are both equal to seven. It can be called a simple equation because it has an equals sign.

Algebra

Algebra is about finding unknown (or mystery) numbers in equations. The unknown numbers are often shown as letters such as a, b, c, x, y, z or symbols such as ✳, ■ or ◆.

You have to find the value of the unknown number to **solve an equation**.

For example:

> Solve $x = 8 - 3$.
>
> x must be equal to the value of the numbers on other side of the equals sign. (8 − 3 is 5). So, $x = 5$.

Sometimes you might see a number next to a letter, for example: $2y$.
It is a short way of saying $2 \times y$.
You might also see, for example, $\frac{10a}{5}$.
It means the same as 10 times a divided by 5, or $10a \div 5$.

> **REMEMBER!**
>
> Notice that **equation** has a similar word root to **equal**, meaning 'the same' or 'identical'.

> **REMEMBER!**
>
> Always use BIDMAS: work out the **B**rackets first, then any **I**ndices, then **D**ivision and/or **M**ultiplication, then **A**ddition and/or **S**ubtraction.

Now look at these examples:

If $x = 2$ and $y = 4$, find $\frac{3x}{6y}$.

$$\frac{3x}{6y} = \frac{3 \times 2}{6 \times 4} = \frac{6}{24} = \frac{1}{4}$$

So $\frac{3x}{6y} = \frac{1}{4}$

If $x = 10$ and $y = 5$, find $\frac{3x}{6y}$.

$$\frac{3x}{6y} = \frac{3 \times 10}{6 \times 5} = \frac{30}{30} = 1$$

So $\frac{3x}{6y} = 1$

When finding an unknown number it can be helpful to use inverse operations so that the unknown number is left on its own on one side of the equation. To do this, look at the sign and do the opposite to **both sides of the equation**.

Look at these examples:

$x - 3 = 9$ What does x equal?

To leave x on its own, **add** 3 to both sides of the equation to remove the ' $- 3$':

$x - 3 + 3 = 9 + 3$

$x = 9 + 3$

$x = 12$

$\frac{a}{5} = 4$ What does x equal?

To leave x on its own, **multiply** both sides of the equation by 5 to remove the '$\div 5$'.

$\frac{a}{5} = 4$

$\frac{a}{5} \times 5 = 4 \times 5$

$a = 20$

You may have to solve equations that need **more than one inverse operation** before the mystery number is left on its own on one side of the equation.

Look at this example:

$10x - 2 = 7x + 4$ What does x equal?

$10x - 2 + 2 = 7x + 4 + 2$

$10x = 7x + 6$

$10x - 7x = 7x + 6 - 7x$

$3x = 6$

$3x \div 3 = 6 \div 3$

$x = 2$

The different inverse operations are given on the next page.

REMEMBER!

Always complete any calculations in brackets first.

Sometimes there are **brackets** in calculations, for example, $3 + (7 - 2)$.

To complete this, you must first do the calculation in the brackets: $7 - 2 = 5$.

The calculation then becomes $3 + 5 = 8$.

Key facts

- $4z = 4 \times z$

- $\frac{3x}{2} = 3x \div 2$

- Whatever you do to one side of an equation you must also do to the other side to keep it equal!

- If you can't work out an answer, try saying the equation out loud using the word 'something' in place of the mystery number – it should make more sense:

  $\frac{42}{b} = 6 \rightarrow$ "42 divided by something equals 6."

⑨ *Function machines*

Function machines

Function machines are diagrams where:

- a number is fed in from the left,
- then one or more boxes tell you to do something to the number using the number operations $(+, \times, -, \div)$
- and then the answer comes out at the right-hand side of the machine.

If the missing number is to the **right** of the function machine, apply the rule or rules that you are given, in turn, to the number on the left and find the missing number.

If the missing number is to the **left** of the function machine, apply the opposite (or **inverse**) of the rule or rules you are given, working backwards to find the missing number.

In this example the missing number is to the left of the function machine and you therefore need to begin with the answer to the right of the machine:

$\rightarrow$ | +9 | ÷4 $\rightarrow$ 7

The two number operations need to be carried out from right to left, using their inverses, so:

The **output** number is 7.

- ÷ 4 becomes × 4: $7 \times 4 = 28$
- + 9 becomes − 9: $28 - 9 = 19$

The **input** is **19**.

You can check your answer by working through the function machine using your answer to begin:

$19 + 9 = 28$

$28 \div 4 = 7$ ✓

Key facts

- Function machines work from left to right. A number is fed in (input) on the left, has number operations operated on it in turn and the answer (output) comes out on the right.

- If the input number is missing, start with the output number and apply the opposite (**inverse**) number operations in order, reading from **right** to **left** to find the answer.

- Always check your answer when you have worked in reverse by going forwards through the function machine.

Fractions and decimals

⑩ *Fractions*

Writing a fraction

"I find fractions confusing."

Talking about **fractions** uses some new long words but they can be easily understood. Think about what is happening when you are using fractions and they will be less confusing.

There are two parts to a simple fraction:

$\frac{1}{2}$ ← the top part is called the numerator
← the bottom part is called the denominator

The denominator tells you how many equal parts the 'something' has been divided, or cut up, into. It also gives the fraction its **name**. 3 = thirds, 5 = fifths, and so on. (We make things complicated by calling 'two-ths' 'halves' and 'fourths' 'quarters'!)

The numerator tells you how many equal parts you are looking at.

Fractions like this are called common fractions.

It can be useful to draw quick pictures of fractions.

For example, to draw diagrams to represent $\frac{1}{8}$, draw one whole shape. You can draw a circle or a box. Divide the shape into **8 equal** pieces. Colour in **one** of the equal pieces.

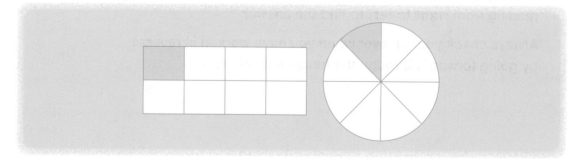

Fractions of numbers

To find a fraction of a number think about how many parts you are making (denominator) and how many of those parts you need (numerator). Divide the number by the denominator and then multiply the answer by the numerator.

For example:

Find $\frac{1}{6}$ of 24.   Find $\frac{5}{6}$ of 24.

$24 \div 6 = 4$ ← divide by the denominator → $24 \div 6 = 4$

$4 \times 1 = 4$ ← multiply by the numerator → $4 \times 5 = 20$

$\frac{1}{6}$ of 24 = 4 $\frac{5}{6}$ of 24 = 20

Mixed numbers

A mixed number is a mixture of a whole number and
a fraction, like $2\frac{1}{2}$ or $7\frac{5}{8}$.

You might be asked to draw diagrams to show mixed numbers:

REMEMBER!

Use your times tables
knowledge when
working out fractions.

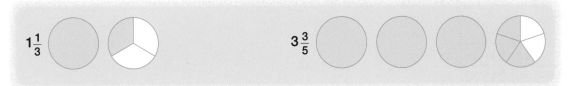

$1\frac{1}{3}$ $3\frac{3}{5}$

Improper fractions

Improper fractions are 'top-heavy' fractions. The numerator is **larger**
than the denominator: $\frac{13}{5}$ $\frac{7}{6}$ $\frac{97}{4}$

Improper fractions can be changed into mixed numbers using division.

- Divide the numerator by the denominator.
- The answer is the whole number.
- The remainder becomes the numerator of the fraction.
  You must keep the denominator the same.

For example:

Change $\frac{13}{5}$ into a mixed number.

$\frac{5}{5}$ $\frac{5}{5}$ $\frac{3}{5}$ $= \frac{13}{5}$

$13 \div 5 = ?$ How many 5s in 13?

$13 \div 5 = 2$ remainder 3

$\frac{13}{5} = 2\frac{3}{5}$

Equivalent fractions

Equivalent fractions are fractions that are **equal** to each other.

For example, two quarters are exactly the same as one half:

$\frac{2}{4} = \frac{1}{2}$

To find a fraction equivalent to another fraction simply multiply the numerator and the denominator by the same number. (See topic 13: Ratio and proportion, page 40.)

For example, $\frac{7}{8}$ is the same as $\frac{14}{16}$, $\frac{21}{24}$, $\frac{28}{32}$, $\frac{35}{40}$.

Can you see why?

Look at this multiplication grid which shows these equivalent fractions.

$\times$	2	3	4	5
7	14	21	28	35
8	16	24	32	40

It can be helpful to draw diagrams.

This diagram compares thirds and sixths:

$\frac{1}{3}$s $\rightarrow$ $\frac{1}{6}$s

It is now easy to see that $\frac{1}{3}$ is equal to $\frac{2}{6}$.

Decimal fractions

(See topic 11: Decimal numbers (page 34))

Comparing and ordering fractions

We can use common sense and our equivalent fraction knowledge to find the largest or smallest fraction and can then order them like this:

Put the following numbers in order of size from smallest to largest.

$$2\frac{1}{3} \qquad 1\frac{1}{2} \qquad \frac{3}{8} \qquad 2\frac{1}{4} \qquad \frac{4}{5}$$

1 Look at the mixed numbers: those with the largest whole number will be the larger numbers.

2 As we are listing these numbers with smallest first, we want to see which is the smaller of $\frac{3}{8}$ and $\frac{4}{5}$.

3 Using 'common sense', we can see that if we divide a shape into eight parts and colour in three parts, we have shaded less than half of the shape. If we divide a shape into five parts and colour in four parts, we have shaded much more than half of the shape. So we know that $\frac{3}{8}$ must be smaller than $\frac{4}{5}$.

4 The next smallest number must be the mixed number with 1 as the whole number.

5 We are left with two mixed numbers with 2 as the whole number. We must compare their fractions to work out which is the smaller. We will use the 'Equivalent fractions' technique to solve this:

$2\frac{1}{4}$ and $2\frac{1}{3}$ have the same whole numbers so we need to compare $\frac{1}{4}$ and $\frac{1}{3}$.

4 and 3 have a common multiple of 12, so we can make 12 the common denominator.

$$\frac{1}{4} = \frac{3}{12} \qquad\qquad \frac{1}{3} = \frac{4}{12}$$

We can see that $\frac{1}{3}$ is the larger fraction because four twelfths is more than three twelfths.

6 Now we can write the numbers in order, from smallest to largest:

$$\frac{3}{8} \qquad \frac{4}{5} \qquad 1\frac{1}{2} \qquad 2\frac{1}{4} \qquad 2\frac{1}{3}$$

REMEMBER!

Whatever number you multiply a denominator by, you must multiply the numerator by the same number to keep the new fraction **equivalent** to the fraction you started with.

Adding and subtracting fractions

Before you work out a calculation which has more than one fraction in a calculation, you need to make sure the denominators are the same.

Look at these examples:

$1\frac{1}{2} + \frac{1}{4} = ?$

1 Convert the mixed number to an improper fraction. $1\frac{1}{2} = \frac{3}{2}$

2 $\frac{3}{2}$ and $\frac{1}{4}$ have different denominators. 4 is a multiple of 2 and of 4.

3 Make the fractions have a denominator of 4. $\frac{3}{2} = \frac{3\times2}{2\times2} = \frac{6}{4}$

$1\frac{1}{2} + \frac{1}{4} = \frac{6}{4} + \frac{1}{4} = \frac{7}{4}$

4 Change the improper fraction to a mixed number. $7 \div 4 = 1$ remainder 3

$\frac{7}{4} = 1\frac{3}{4}$

$1\frac{1}{2} + \frac{1}{4} = 1\frac{3}{4}$

Don't forget that it can be helpful to draw diagrams when working out fractions.

$2 - \frac{3}{4} = ?$

1 Change 2 into quarters. $2 = \frac{2}{1} = \frac{8}{4}$

2 $\frac{8}{4} - \frac{3}{4} = \frac{5}{4}$

3 Change the improper fraction to a mixed number. $5 \div 4 = 1$ remainder 1

$\frac{5}{4} = 1\frac{1}{4}$

$2 - \frac{3}{4} = 1\frac{1}{4}$

REMEMBER!

Sometimes it helps to say the calculation in words: '**eight** quarters take away **three** quarters equals **five** quarters'.

Simplifying fractions

To understand what fractions mean we usually write them as simply as possible. The fraction $\frac{42}{56}$ is difficult to understand. We make it as simple as possible by reducing it to its simplest or lowest terms.

To do this, find a number that will divide exactly into both the numerator and the denominator (a common factor). Keep doing this until the equivalent fraction is as simple as possible (the numbers are as small as possible).

For example:

> Reduce $\frac{42}{56}$ to its simplest terms.
>
> 42 and 56 have a common factor of 7. $\qquad$ $42 \div 7 = 6,\ 56 \div 7 = 8$
>
> $$\frac{42}{56} = \frac{6}{8}$$
>
> 6 and 8 have a common factor of 2. $\qquad$ $6 \div 2 = 3,\ 8 \div 2 = 4$
>
> $$\frac{6}{8} = \frac{3}{4}$$
>
> $\frac{42}{56}$ is $\frac{3}{4}$ in simplest terms.

This is sometimes called cancelling.

$$\frac{42 \ ^{6^3}}{56 \ _{8_4}} = \frac{3}{4}$$

First divide the top and bottom by 7, then divide top and bottom by 2. When there are no more common factors to divide by you have found the fraction in its simplest form.

Multiplying fractions

We can multiply fractions by multiplying the numerators together, multiplying the denominators together and then writing our answer in its simplest form like this:

> $$\frac{2}{3} \times \frac{3}{8} \qquad \begin{matrix}(2 \times 3 = 6)\\[4pt](3 \times 8 = 24)\end{matrix} \implies \frac{6}{24} = \frac{1}{4}$$
>
> **We have found two-thirds of three-eighths.**

REMEMBER!

$\frac{2}{3} \times \frac{3}{8}$ is the same as

$\frac{2}{3}$ **of** $\frac{3}{8}$.

This diagram shows a different way to look at this calculation:

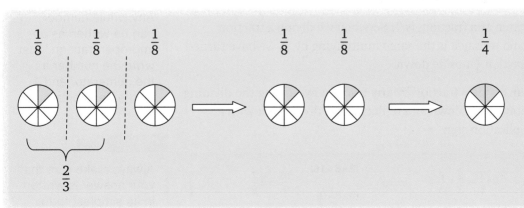

We can also use cancelling to keep the numbers smaller:

$$\frac{2}{3} \times \frac{3}{3} = \frac{2^1 \times 3^1}{3_1 \times 8_4} = \frac{1}{4}$$

1 **Divide the 3s in the numerator and denominator by 3 (= 1).**
2 **Divide the 2 (numerator number) and 8 (denominator number) by 2 (= 1 and = 4).**
3 **Multiply the numerator numbers (1 × 1), and the denominator numbers (1 × 4) to get the fraction $\frac{1}{4}$.**

> **REMEMBER!**
>
> Dividing the numerator and denominator by the same number gives you a simpler equivalent fraction.

Dividing fractions

Dividing fractions by whole numbers

What happens when you divide by two? You find **half** of something.

What happens when you divide by four? You find **a quarter** of something.

So ÷ 2 is the same as × $\frac{1}{2}$ and ÷ 4 is the same as × $\frac{1}{4}$.

This is true for any whole number ... ÷ 498 is the same as × $\frac{1}{498}$!

> **REMEMBER!**
>
> When you look at a fraction, you can read the line as 'divided by' or 'out of', like a score. So $\frac{3}{8}$ is the same as three divided by eight or three out of eight.

$$\frac{2}{3} \div 4 \implies \frac{2}{3} \times \frac{1}{4} \implies \begin{array}{c}(2 \times 1 = 2)\\(3 \times 4 = 12)\end{array} \quad \frac{2}{12} = \frac{1}{6}$$

or $\quad \frac{2}{3} \div 4 = \frac{2}{3} \times \frac{1}{4} = \frac{2^1}{3} \times \frac{1}{4_2} = \frac{1}{6}$

Dividing fractions by fractions

4, written as a fraction, is $\frac{4}{1}$. So when we divide a fraction by 4 and we say it is the same multiplying by $\frac{1}{4}$, we have turned the fraction $\frac{4}{1}$ upside down.

We can divide a fraction by **any** fraction by turning the dividing fraction upside down and replacing the divide sign with a multiplication sign.

> **REMEMBER!**
>
> Any whole number can be written as an improper fraction. Just write the number as the numerator and 1 as the denominator.

> **REMEMBER!**
>
> Always make sure that your answer is written in its simplest form.

$$\frac{2}{3} \div \frac{3}{8} = \frac{2}{3} \times \frac{8}{3} \implies \begin{array}{c}(2 \times 8 = 16)\\(3 \times 3 = 9)\end{array} \quad \frac{16}{9} = 1\frac{7}{9}$$

Dividing fractions by whole numbers:

We can also divide a fraction by a whole number by turning our whole number into a fraction with a 1 as the denominator and then using the same strategy, like this:

$$\frac{2}{3} \div 4 \implies \frac{2}{3} \div \frac{4}{1} = \frac{2}{3} \times \frac{1}{4} \quad \begin{array}{l} (2 \times 1 = 2) \\ \\ (3 \times 4 = 12) \end{array} \implies \frac{2}{12} = \frac{1}{6}$$

Key facts

- $\dfrac{3}{4} \begin{array}{l} \leftarrow \text{numerator} \\ \leftarrow \text{denominator} \end{array}$

- The numerator and denominator in a **common fraction** are both whole numbers.

- To find a **fraction of a number**, divide the number by the denominator and then multiply the answer by the numerator.

- A **mixed number** is a mixture of a whole number and a fraction: $1\frac{3}{4}$

- An **improper fraction** has a larger numerator than denominator: $\frac{9}{2}$

- **Equivalent fractions** are equal to each other: $\frac{1}{3} = \frac{2}{6}$ or $\frac{9}{27} = \frac{30}{90}$

- Before completing a calculation with more than one fraction, make the denominators the same.

- To reduce a fraction to its **simplest** or **lowest terms**, divide the numerator and denominator by their highest common factor (see topic 5: Factors and multiples page 16).

Exam tips

In an exam, remember

- to put fractions into their simplest or lowest form,
- strategies such as
  - 'find a common denominator for adding and subtracting fractions'
  - 'turn the last fraction upside down then multiply' when dividing fractions.

(11) Decimal numbers

Decimal fractions

"What does 'decimal fractions' mean?"

When we write a decimal number, we put a dot to the right of the digit in the ones column.

The digits to the left of the decimal point represent whole numbers: ones, tens, hundreds, thousands, and so on.

The digits to the right of the decimal point represent parts of one whole: tenths ($\frac{1}{10}$s), hundredths ($\frac{1}{100}$s), thousandths ($\frac{1}{1000}$s), and so on.

The decimal point separates whole numbers from numbers that are fractions between zero and one.

The digits to the right of the decimal point are a decimal fraction. An example of a decimal fraction is the number 0.256.

It is made up of $\frac{2}{10} + \frac{50}{100} + \frac{6}{1000}$ and is equal to $\frac{256}{1000}$.

You can remind yourself about the value of digits in different columns by looking back at topic 1: Place value, page 6.

> **REMEMBER!**
>
> Decimal fractions always have a decimal point.

Converting between decimal and common fractions

It is useful to know some decimal fractions and their common fraction equivalents. These are listed below:

$\frac{1}{10} = 0.1$ $\frac{2}{10} = \frac{1}{5} = 0.2$ $\frac{3}{10} = 0.3$

$\frac{4}{10} = \frac{2}{5} = 0.4$ $\frac{5}{10} = \frac{1}{2} = 0.5$ $\frac{6}{10} = \frac{3}{5} = 0.6$

$\frac{7}{10} = 0.7$ $\frac{8}{10} = \frac{4}{5} = 0.8$ $\frac{9}{10} = 0.9$ $\frac{10}{10} = 1.0$

$\frac{25}{100} = \frac{1}{4} = 0.25$ $\frac{50}{100} = \frac{2}{4} = \frac{1}{2} = 0.5$ $\frac{75}{100} = \frac{3}{4} = 0.75$

If you need to change a common fraction to a decimal fraction, it is very useful to remember that a common fraction can be thought of as a division calculation.

Look at this example:

Work out $\frac{3}{8}$ as a decimal fraction.

$\frac{3}{8}$ means $3 \div 8$ or $3.0000 \div 8$

We can estimate that the answer will be less than 0.5 because $\frac{3}{8}$ is less than $\frac{4}{8}$ which is equivalent to $\frac{1}{2}$ or 0.5.

$$\begin{array}{r} 0.3 \\ \hline 8\,|\,3.0^60000... \end{array} \qquad \begin{array}{r} 0.3\;7 \\ \hline 8\,|\,3.0^60^40\,00... \end{array} \qquad \begin{array}{r} 0.3\;7\;5 \\ \hline 8\,|\,3.0^60^40\,00... \end{array}$$

So, $\frac{3}{8}$ = 0.375

REMEMBER!

Estimate your answer first, so that the decimal point doesn't end up in the wrong place.

Sometimes you will have to change decimal fractions to common fractions or mixed numbers. It is important to think carefully about tenths, hundredths and thousandths. See topic 1: Place value, page 6, to remind yourself which column represents each of these.

REMEMBER!

You can write as many zeros as you like at the end of a decimal number. For example, 0.23 is the same as 0.23000000... and 12.4 is the same as 12.4000000...

The digits to the left of the decimal point (whole numbers) don't need to be changed to write a decimal number as a mixed number.

Digits to the right of the decimal point are the numerator in the fraction part of the mixed number.

For example, if there is one digit to the right of the decimal point, then that digit represents the number of tenths:

$$3.7 = 3\frac{7}{10}$$

If there are two digits to the right of the decimal point, then those digits represent the number of hundredths:

$$3.75 = 3\frac{75}{100}$$

Similarly, if there are three digits to the right of the decimal point, then those digits represent the number of thousandths:

$$3.758 = 3\frac{758}{1000}$$

It is important to make sure your fraction is in its simplest terms, so $3\frac{75}{100}$ can be simplified to become $3\frac{3}{4}$. See topic 10: Fractions, page 26, to remind yourself how to simplify fractions.

To arrange a group of decimal fractions in order, write them out one above the other, making sure the decimal points are all lined up above each other.

Look at this example:

> Write these numbers in order, smallest to largest: 3.241, 3.124, 3.412, 3.214, 3.421, 3.142
>
> 1 The whole numbers are the same, so begin by looking at the tenths column.
> 2 To order from the smallest first, look for the smallest tenths digit (1).
> 3 There are two numbers with 1 tenth, so look at the hundredths column to find the smaller of the two numbers. 3.124 is smaller than 3.142.
> 4 Now look for the next-largest digits in the tenths column.
> 5 There are two numbers with 2 tenths, so look at the hundredths column to find the smaller of the two numbers. 3.214 is smaller than 3.241.
> 6 Now look for the next-largest digits in the tenths column.
> 7 There are two numbers with 4 tenths, so look at the hundredths column to find the smaller of the two numbers. 3.412 is smaller than 3.421.
>
> 3.241
> 3.124
> 3.412
> 3.214
> 3.421
> 3.142
>
> The numbers in order are: 3.124, 3.142, 3.214, 3.241, 3.412, 3.421.

Add, subtract, multiply and divide decimal numbers

You will need to know how to add, subtract, multiply and divide decimal numbers in 11+ Maths.

Decimals can be added and subtracted in exactly the same way as whole numbers.

Keep a clear idea of what each of the digits means by reminding yourself of the place value columns (see topic 1: Place value, page 6). It can be helpful to write the numbers you are adding or subtracting one underneath the other, always keeping the decimal point in the same column:

$$
\begin{array}{r}
3.64 \\
+\ \ 5.29 \\
\hline
8.93 \\
\hline
\end{array}
\qquad
\begin{array}{r}
7.65 \\
-\ \ 2.42 \\
\hline
5.23 \\
\hline
\end{array}
$$

To multiply decimal fractions, it can be useful to remember to say "of" when you see a × sign.

For example:

In the calculation 0.2×0.2, you could ask yourself:

"What is two tenths of two tenths?"

First, find one tenth of 0.2 by dividing 0.2 by 10 (move the digits 1 column to the right) and then double it to find two tenths.

$0.2 \div 10 = 0.02$ $\qquad$ $0.02 \times 2 = 0.04$

Or you can just ignore the decimal points to begin with, multiply $2 \times 2 = 4$ and then say:

"There were two decimal places, so I have to put those back in my answer now":

$0.2 \times 0.2 = 0.04$

To divide by a decimal fraction, it can be helpful to think of the decimal fraction as a common fraction.

For example:

In the calculation $5 \div 0.5$, call 0.5 a half and say:

"How many halves in 5?"

There are two halves in one, so there are 5×2, or 10 halves in 5.

$5 \div 0.5 = 10$

For questions where the decimal fraction isn't an obvious common fraction, then saying the question out loud can still help. For example, $6 \div 1.2$ can be said as "How many 1.2s in 6?"

The question can then be solved using repeated addition:

$1.2 + 1.2 + 1.2 + 1.2 + 1.2 = 6$, therefore $6 \div 1.2 = 5$

Key facts

- 0.37 is an example of a decimal fraction.

- In a decimal fraction the digits to the right of the decimal point represent a fraction between zero and one. It can be shown as tenths, hundredths, thousandths, and so on.

- A common fraction can be changed into a decimal fraction using division. $\frac{3}{8} \rightarrow 3 \div 8 = 0.375$

- A decimal number can be changed into a mixed number: $3.75 = 3\frac{75}{100} = 3\frac{3}{4}$

- Decimal numbers can be used in addition, subtraction, multiplication and division calculations.

(12) *Percentages*

"I keep forgetting what the word 'percentage' means."

Per means '**out of**', **cent** means '**100**' (there are 100 centimetres in a metre; a century is 100 years; there are 100 cents in a dollar).

These are some important percentages you should recognise:

- $100\% = \frac{100}{100} = 1$ (one whole)
- $75\% = \frac{75}{100} = \frac{3}{4}$ (three quarters)
- $50\% = \frac{50}{100} = \frac{1}{2}$ (one half)
- $25\% = \frac{25}{100} = \frac{1}{4}$ (one quarter)
- $10\% = \frac{10}{100} = \frac{1}{10}$ (one tenth)

You know how easy it is to divide by 10 (see topic 1: Place value, page 6), so 10% is a particularly useful percentage for working things out.

30%
($\div 10$, then $\times 3$)

60%
($\div 10$, then $\times 6$)

20%
($\div 10$, then $\times 2$)

10%
Divide by 10

$2\frac{1}{2}\%$
is half of 5% so
($\div 10$, then $\div 2$, then $\div 2$)

15%
is 10% + 5% so find 10%,
then 5% and add them together

5%
is half of 10% so
($\div 10$, then $\div 2$)

Look at this example:

Find 40% of 320.
1	Divide by 10 to find 10%.	$320 \div 10 = 32$
2	Multiply by 4 to find 40%.	$32 \times 4 = 128$
		40% of 320 = 128

To **increase** a given amount by a percentage, you find the given percentage and **add** it on to the original amount.

To **decrease** a given amount by a percentage, you find the given percentage and **subtract** it from the original amount.

For example:

What is the price of a £25 pair of jeans with 20% off in the sale?
1	Find 10% of the price.	$£25.00 \div 10 = £2.50$
2	20% is $2 \times 10\%$ so double the amount.	$£2.50 \times 2 = £5.00$
3	Take 20% **off** the original price.	$£25.00 - £5.00 = £20$

The new price is £20.

Key facts

- Percentages are all based on something being divided into 100 equal parts. 100% of something means all of it; 50% means one half of it; and 25% means one quarter of it.

- To find 1% of an amount, divide it by 100.

- For 11+ Maths you can work out most percentages by finding 10% first.

⑬ Ratio and proportion

Ratio

A ratio shows how a total amount can be shared out in unequal parts. A colon between two or more numbers is used to show ratio in maths, for example 3:2.

The picture shows red and white beads in the ratio 3:2. We say this as "three to two".

There are 3 red beads to every 2 white beads. We could also say "3 red beads for every 2 white beads".

When you share something in a given ratio, you must first total the numbers in the ratio to find out how many equal parts you need to work with. This is like finding out the denominator in a fraction.

We can also write ratios with more than two numbers. So, 4:5:6 might describe a recipe where you need 4 mushrooms for every 5 tomatoes and 6 eggs.

Or it might be a way of sharing money between three sisters. There are 15 parts altogether (4 + 5 + 6) so £15 would be shared in the ratio £4:£5:£6. If the sisters were sharing 45p, each part would be 3p (45 ÷ 15) and they would get 4 × 3p:5 × 3p:6 × 3p or 12p:15p:18p.

Proportion

If the ratio of 3 red beads to every 2 white beads is used to arrange 5 beads in a pattern, then the proportion of red beads is 3, or **3 in every 5**, and the proportion of white beads is 2, or **2 in every 5**:

$\frac{3}{5}$ of the beads are red, $\frac{2}{5}$ of the beads are white.

"3 in every 5" can be written as the fraction $\frac{3}{5}$ and "2 in every 5" can be written as the fraction $\frac{2}{5}$.

> **REMEMBER!**
> To describe a ratio say **"to"** or **"to** every".

> **REMEMBER!**
> A **ratio** is used to **compare two or more numbers or quantities**.

> **REMEMBER!**
> To describe a proportion it can be helpful to say **"in** every".

> **REMEMBER!**
> When you share out an amount using a given ratio, then each share is a **proportion** of the total **amount**.

Look at these examples:

£4.80 is shared between Adam, Aisha and Bethany in the ratio 3:1:2.
What **proportion** of the money does Bethany receive?

1 Find the total number of equal parts.

$$3 + 1 + 2 = 6$$

2 Bethany is third in the list of names so she gets the third portion of the ratio.

3 She gets 2 out of 6 parts.

$$2 \text{ out of } 6 = \frac{2}{6} = \frac{1}{3}$$

Bethany gets $\frac{1}{3}$ of the money.

£4.80 is shared between Adam, Aisha and Bethany in the ratio 3:1:2.
What **amount** of money does Bethany receive?

1 Find the total number of equal parts.

$$3 + 1 + 2 = 6$$

2 Divide the amount to be shared by the number of equal parts.

$$£4.80 \div 6 = £0.80$$

3 Each part is worth £0.80.

4 Bethany is third in the list of names so she gets the third number of parts.

5 She gets 2 parts.

$$£0.80 \times 2 = £1.60$$

Bethany receives £1.60.

Scale factor

If we imagine drawing a picture of our hand, we would use a whole piece
of A4 paper to draw around our hand, fingers and thumb. If we wanted to
draw our whole body, we would be joining lots of pieces of paper together.
It wouldn't be very practical! Instead, we can represent our body by using a
scale. We might use 1 cm on the paper to represent 10 cm of our body. We
would write this scale as 1:10.

We commonly use scaling for recording distances on maps and in atlases,
for sewing patterns, for architecture plans and for any occasion when we
need accuracy.

Look at these examples:

My map has a scale of 1:150 000.
How far is it from my house to the airport if it measures 6 cm on the map?

1 cm on the map represents 150 000 cm on the ground.

1 cm on the map represents 1500 m on the ground (divide by 100 to turn centimetres into metres).

1 cm on the map represents 1.5 km on the ground (divide by 1000 to turn metres into kilometres).

6 cm on the map represents 6 × 1.5 km = 9 km.
It is 9 km from the house to the airport.

I am travelling 36 km. How many centimetres will this be on the map?

1 cm on the map represents 1.5 km on the ground.

How many 1.5s are there in 36? There are two in 3, so 20 in 30 and 4 in 6, a total of 24.

36 km on the ground will measure 24 cm on the map.

Key facts

- A **ratio** is used to **compare two numbers or quantities**.

- Ratio is said as "**to** every" or "for every" and is written using a colon between the parts, for example 2:1. This is the ratio "2 to 1".

- When you share out an amount using a given ratio, then each share is a **proportion** of the total amount.

- Proportion is a fraction of the whole amount.

- You might be asked to find the **proportion** (the fraction or percentage) of an amount shared, or the **amount** someone gets when something is shared.

Handling data

⑭ *Organising and comparing information*

Data

Data can be numbers or values or words and is usually collected by observing, questioning or measuring. In 11+ Maths you need to be able to understand different ways of showing data, such as line graphs, block graphs, pie charts, tables of information and Venn diagrams.

You also need to be able to answer questions about data shown in these ways. If you have to draw graphs or charts yourself, you must be very careful to choose a sensible way of showing the numbers from your data. Organising your information into tables may show patterns or similarities in your data.

> **REMEMBER!**
>
> **Data** is the word that describes collections of information.

> **REMEMBER!**
>
> In this book, whenever a new maths word is introduced, it is printed in red. If you need to, you can check its meaning in the Glossary at the back of the book.

Graphs

Graphs can have bars, lines or pictures representing the data.

Every graph has two lines, the x-axis and y-axis (plural: axes), which join or intersect at the point (0, 0), which we call the origin, like this:

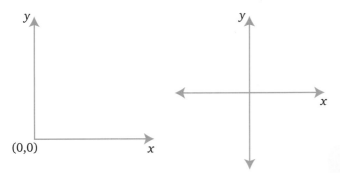

> **REMEMBER!**
>
> A **graph** is a type of picture that shows data.

In maths, x and y are mystery amounts and you must label the axes to make it clear what they represent.

The x-axis is always horizontal (straight across, like the horizon).

The y-axis is always **vertical** (straight up and down).

Look at the bar graph. It shows the percentage of children in a school who own different pets.

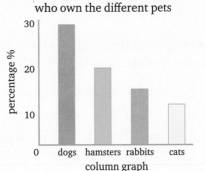

Percentage of children in a school who own the different pets

column graph

Pie charts

A pie chart is a circle divided into sections to show how something is shared or divided into groups. Look at this pie chart:

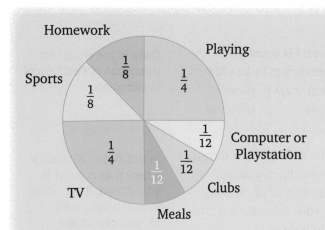

It shows how much time children in Year 6 spend doing different activities between 4 p.m. and 8 p.m.

From the chart, we can see, for example, that they spend $\frac{1}{8}$ of their time doing homework, $\frac{1}{4}$ of their time playing and $\frac{1}{12}$ of their time going to clubs.

The following facts can help you answer many questions about pie charts.

- 360° represents 100% = 1

- 180° represents 50% = $\frac{1}{2}$

- 90° represents 25% = $\frac{1}{4}$

- 270° represents 75% = $\frac{3}{4}$

- 45° represents $12\frac{1}{2}$% = $\frac{1}{8}$

> **REMEMBER!**
>
> There are 360° in a circle, 180° in a semicircle and 90° in a right angle.

Look again at the pie chart above. What percentage of their time do the children spend watching TV and doing sports?

A quarter of the pie chart represents TV, so they watch TV for 25% of the time.

An eighth of the pie chart represents sports, so they do sport for $12\frac{1}{2}$% of the time.

Decision trees

Decision trees are a useful way of organising information that can show us every possible outcome of a decision based on clear questions.

Imagine you have this selection of chocolates:

strawberry cream   dark almond bite   pure dark chocolate

nut toffee   dark chocolate mint   white minty layer

I want to work out which chocolate is your favourite, but you can only answer 'yes' or 'no' to my questions. What questions should I ask?
I could ask:

Is it dark chocolate? Does it include a nut? Does it contain mint?

Here is a decision tree to make it easier for me to work out your favourite chocolate.

Complete the missing questions in the boxes below.

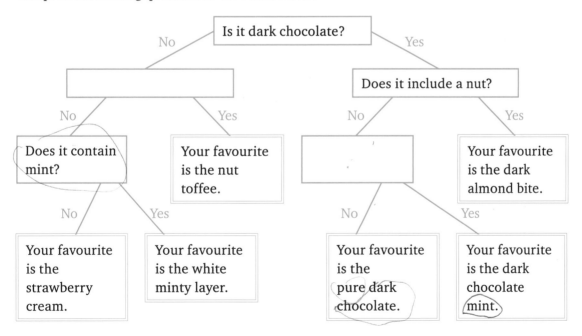

1 Once we have said 'yes' or 'no' to dark chocolate we are then asking if the chocolate contains a nut. As this is written on the right-hand side box, we need to add the same wording on the left-hand box. This means that the chocolates could be:

  a Dark chocolate with a nut

  b Dark chocolate without a nut

  c Not dark chocolate, with a nut

  d Not dark chocolate, without a nut

2 The next level down determines if the chocolate contains mint. As the box on the left-hand side asks 'Does it contain mint?' we need to write the same question in the right-hand side box. This means that the chocolates could be:

  a Dark chocolate (with or without nuts) with mint

  b Dark chocolate (with or without nuts) without mint

  c Not dark chocolate (with or without nuts) with mint

  d Not dark chocolate (with or without nuts) without mint

All the chocolates appear once (and only once) at the end of a branch of the tree.

Answering 'yes' or 'no' to each question means I can find out which is your favourite.

Venn diagrams

Each ring is labelled to show which items of data can be included in it and which cannot. Where two or more rings overlap, the data that can be included in both or all rings is written in the overlapped section.

> **REMEMBER!**
>
> **Venn diagrams** are diagrams in which the data is organised into rings.

The table shows the type of pets that 25 children in Year 6 have:

Pet	Number of children
Dogs	6
Cats	12
Other pets	8
No pets	6

This data is shown in a Venn diagram and gives us some more information.

Six children have no pets, so 19 children should be on the main part of the diagram. 18 are shown, so one child had dogs, cats and another pet.

We can check this by seeing the Venn diagram shows us six children with dogs, 12 children with cats and eight children with other pets.

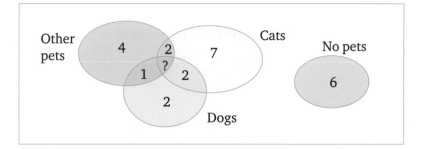

(15) *Mean, median, mode and range*

REMEMBER!

An average is a value that is a typical value in a set of data.

Mean, median and mode

There are three different types of average of a set of data: the mean, the median and the mode.

The **mean** is found by adding together all the numbers or values in the set of data and dividing by how many numbers there are in the set.

The **median** is the middle number or value when the numbers in the set are put in order of size. If there are two middle numbers, you find the mean of those two numbers by adding them up and dividing by two. This is the median.

The **mode** is the number or value in the data that comes up most often.

Range

The range of a set of numbers or values is the difference between the smallest number and the largest number.

Look at this example:

Find the range, mode, median and mean for this set of test results:

7	10	7	5	9	9	10	6	9

Range: Highest score is 10, lowest score is 5 $10 - 5 = 5$

The range is 5.

Mode: 9 appears more times than any other score.

The mode is 9

Median: We need to arrange the scores in order:

5	6	7	7	**9**	9	9	10	10

The middle number is 9 so the median is 9.

Mean: $5 + 6 + 7 + 7 + 9 + 9 + 9 + 10 + 10 = 72$

There are nine scores with a total of 72. $72 \div 9 = 8$

The mean is 8.

Key facts

- **Average** – A value that is a typical value in a set of data.
- **Range** – the difference between the largest and the smallest value.
- **Mode** – the value that appears the most often.
- **Median** – the value in the middle when put in size order.
- **Mean** – the result of dividing the total of all the values by the number of values. It is often just called the average of a set of numbers.

⑯ Probability

The probability of something happening is the likelihood or chance of it happening.

If something is certain to happen, its probability is 1.

If something is impossible, its probability is 0.

If an event is neither certain, nor impossible, then its probability is somewhere between zero and one and is often written as a fraction.

REMEMBER!

Probability means 'chance' or 'possibility'.

For example, imagine tossing a coin and it landing heads up. There is a 1 in 2 chance of this happening, so its probability is:

The number of correct outcomes $\longrightarrow$ 1 $\longleftarrow$ Heads: only 1 correct outcome
The number of possible outcomes $\longrightarrow$ 2 $\longleftarrow$ Heads or Tails: 2 possible outcomes

Sometimes, as with throwing two dice, there may be many different combinations that are possible.

Each die (or dice) has six numbers, so when throwing two dice you have 6 × 6 possibilities: 36 in all. There is only one way to score a total of 2 with two dice, so the probability of scoring 2 with two dice is 1 in 36 or $\frac{1}{36}$.

Look at this example:

> **REMEMBER!**
>
> It can be helpful to write down all the possibilities before working out a probability but be methodical so that you are sure to get all the combinations!

If you roll two dice, what is the probability that the total score is 6?

Here are the ways you could score 6:

The total 6 can be made in 6 different ways. There are 36 scores, so the probability of the total being 6 is $\frac{6}{36} = \frac{1}{6}$.

Dice 1	Dice 2
1	5
5	1
2	4
4	2
3	3
3	3

In 11+ Maths, you may have to find the probability of picking balls or numbers out of a bag, throwing a die or dice, tossing coins or choosing playing cards from a pack.

With dice or coins, it is possible to have weighted or unfair ones, so very often a question will tell you that the dice or coins are fair. It means all the possible outcomes are equally likely.

> **REMEMBER!**
>
> A pack of playing cards has four suits: hearts, diamonds, clubs and spades.
>
> Each suit has 13 cards: ace (1), 2, 3, 4, 5, 6, 7, 8, 9, 10, jack, queen and king.
>
> Altogether there are 52 cards.

Key facts

- The **probability** of something happening is the likelihood or chance of it happening.
- A probability of 1 means an event is certain to happen.
- A probability of 0 means an event is impossible or certain not to happen.
- All other probabilities are given as a fraction between 0 and 1.

Shape and space

(17) *2D shapes: circles, angles and bearings*

Circles

You need to know the names of certain parts of a circle:

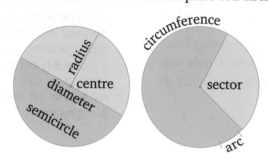

Concentric circles share the same centre point but the radius of each circle is different.

It is important to know the relationship between the diameter and radius of a circle:

the diameter is two times the radius. $d = 2 \times r$

the radius is half the diameter $r = \frac{1}{2}$ of d or $\frac{d}{2}$

A circle has an infinite (never-ending) number of radii (or radiuses) and an infinite number of diameters, which means that you can draw a radius or a diameter anywhere on a circle as long as it goes from the circumference to or through the centre of the circle.

An arc is part of the circumference. A sector is part of a circle, between two radii and an arc.

Angles

An angle tells us how far something turns or rotates.

Angles are measured in degrees. There are 360 degrees (360°) in a full turn.

When a circle is divided into quarters, four **right angles** (90°) are made. This is the same as a quarter turn.

It is very important that you recognise a right angle. It looks like the corner of a square or a piece of paper.

An angle of 180° is a straight line. It can be thought of as two right angles (90°) together. Your protractor will probably have 180° as its largest amount. It is half a complete turn or the angle in a semicircle.

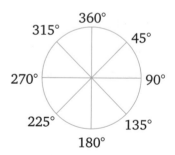

Angles less than 90° are called acute. Acute means **sharp**.

Angles greater than 90° but less than 180° are called obtuse. Obtuse means **blunt**.

Angles greater than 180° are called reflex.

Every right angle, acute angle or obtuse angle has a matching or complementary reflex angle. The two angles add up to 360°, a complete turn.

To measure angles accurately you need to be able to use a protractor, a maths tool consisting of a transparent semicircle with two scales, one clockwise and one anticlockwise, each with the degrees between 0 and 180 marked on it (see topic 26: Reading scales (page 68)).

Two lines are perpendicular if they are at right angles to each other. One line is perpendicular to the other.

Line AC is at right angles to line BC.   Line AC is perpendicular to line BD.

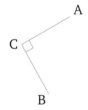   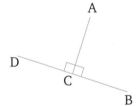

Two lines are parallel if they travel in the same direction and are the same distance apart all along their lengths.

Parallel lines never meet and therefore will never make an angle between them.

Parallel lines do not have to be the same length.

Parallel lines do not have to be straight. Think of railway tracks!

Bearings

This diagram shows the main directions marked on a compass:

A bearing is the angle between the direction north and the direction in which something is travelling. We always measure bearings clockwise from north.

See how the compass points match the degrees shown on the circle. These are the bearing measurements for the eight main compass points.

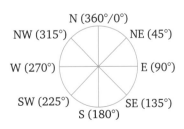

Key facts

- There are 360° in a full turn.
- An **acute angle** is less than 90°.
- A **right angle** is 90°.
- An **obtuse angle** is between 90° and 180°.
- A **reflex angle** is greater than 180°.
- **Perpendicular lines** are at right angles to each other.
- **Parallel lines** never meet but run the same distance apart from each other for their entire length.
- A **compass** is used to find a **bearing**: the angle between north and the direction in which something is travelling.
- The eight main points on a compass are N, NE, E, SE, S, SW, W and NW.

⑱ *2D shapes: triangles*

Types of triangle

"Triangles all look very similar to me."

Triangles can be lots of different shapes but they all have three sides and three angles.

They are named according to their sides and sorted into different groups:

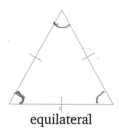

equilateral

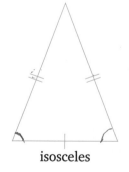

isosceles

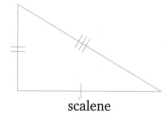

scalene

An equilateral triangle has **three equal sides** and three equal angles.

An isosceles triangle has **two equal sides** and two equal angles.

A scalene triangle has **no equal sides** and no equal angles.

Notice how the sides can be labelled with short lines to show
how they compare with each other.

Triangles can also be named according to their angles:

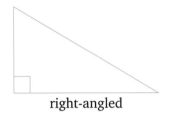

right-angled

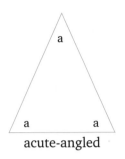

acute-angled

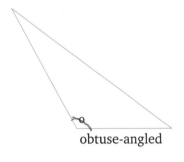

obtuse-angled

A right-angled triangle has **one right angle**.

An acute-angled triangle has **three acute angles**.

An obtuse-angled triangle has **one obtuse angle**.

Area of a triangle

To find the area of any triangle: imagine it in a rectangle. It fills half
the space of the rectangle. Find the area of the rectangle and then halve
that amount.

Area $= \frac{1}{2} \times$ (base × height) or $A = \frac{1}{2}(b \times h)$

The area of a triangle (A) is its base (b) multiplied by its height (h), all
divided by 2.

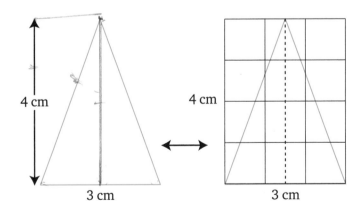

The area of this triangle is:

$$\frac{1}{2} \times 3 \text{ cm} \times 4 \text{ cm} = 6 \text{ cm}^2$$

See topic 20: Perimeter and area (page 56) for a description of the units of
measurement used to represent area.

Key facts

- **Equilateral** triangle – three equal sides and angles.
- **Isosceles** triangle – two equal sides and angles.
- **Scalene** triangle – no equal sides or angles.
- **Right-angled** triangle – one right angle.
- **Acute-angled** triangle – three acute angles.
- **Obtuse-angled** triangle – one obtuse angle.
- Area of a triangle = $\frac{1}{2}$(base × height).

⑲ *2D shapes: quadrilaterals and other polygons*

Quadrilaterals

Quadrilaterals have four sides and also have four angles.

If you join up the opposite angles of a quadrilateral, you form its diagonals.

You need to know the names and properties of these quadrilaterals:

> **REMEMBER!**
>
> The term **quadrilateral** can be used for all four-sided 2D shapes.

- A **square** has four equal sides, four right angles and four lines of symmetry.

- A rhombus also has four equal sides, but two equal acute angles, two equal obtuse angles and two lines of symmetry.

- A **rectangle** has two pairs of parallel sides of equal length, four right angles and two lines of symmetry. Rectangles are sometimes called oblongs.

- A parallelogram has two pairs of parallel sides, two equal acute angles and two equal obtuse angles. It has no lines of symmetry.

- A **kite** has <u>two pairs of equal-length sides</u> that are adjacent, or next to each other. It has one pair of opposite equal angles and <u>one line of symmetry</u>.

- A **trapezium** looks like a triangle with its head chopped off! Two of its sides are parallel.

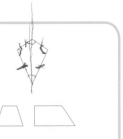

"The names of some of these four-sided shapes are hard to remember."

This is where a mnemonic may help. Try making up a rhyme or silly story to help you learn the names and practise drawing and labelling the different types of quadrilaterals until you know them.

Polygons

The sides of a regular polygon are the same length and all angles are equal. An irregular polygon has sides and angles that are not the same.

> **REMEMBER!**
>
> A **polygon** is any 2D shape with three or more straight sides.

You need to know the names of these regular polygons and to be able to recognise them:

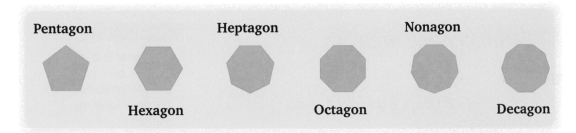

Pentagon   Heptagon   Nonagon

Hexagon   Octagon   Decagon

A pentagon has **five** sides.

A hexagon has **six** sides.

A heptagon has **seven** sides.

An octagon has **eight** sides.

The cross-section of some pencils is hexagonal.

A 50p coin is a heptagon.

An **oct**opus has eight tentacles and in music, an **oct**ave is eight notes in a scale.

> **REMEMBER!**
>
> The more sides a polygon has, the more it resembles a circle.

A nonagon has **nine** sides.

A decagon has **ten** sides.

Key facts

- **Quadrilaterals** are four-sided 2D shapes.
- **Polygons** are 2D shapes with three or more straight sides.
- The sides of a **regular polygon** are the same length and all angles are equal. All other polygons are irregular.
- Polygons are named according to the number of sides:

Name of polygon	Number of sides
triangle	3
quadrilateral	4
pentagon	5
hexagon	6
heptagon	7
octagon	8
nonagon	9
decagon	10

(20) Perimeter and area

Perimeter

The perimeter of a 2D shape is the total distance round the edges of the shape.

To find the perimeter of this rectangle, add all the measurements of the sides together.

5 cm + 3 cm + 5 cm + 3 cm = 16 cm

The perimeter of this shape is 16 cm.

A quick way to work out the perimeter of a shape is to use multiplication. For example, for this rectangle you could double the length and add it to double the width:

> **REMEMBER!**
>
> Perimeter is a length; it might be measured in millimetres (mm), centimetres (cm), metres (m) or kilometres (km).

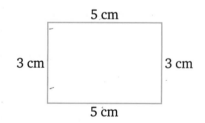

56

perimeter = (2 × length) + (2 × width) $p = 2l + 2w$

$2l = 2 \times 5 = 10$ cm

$2w = 2 \times 3 = 6$ cm

so, perimeter = 16 cm

To find the perimeter of an irregular shape, find a starting point and add up the lengths of all sides until you get back to the starting point.

Area

The **area** of a 2D shape is the space inside the perimeter, which could be coloured in.

REMEMBER!

Area is a measurement of space covered. It might be measured in: square centimetres (cm^2) for small areas, square metres (m^2) for large expanses like football pitches, or square kilometres (km^2) for vast expanses such as countries.

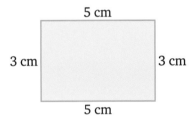

To find the area of this rectangle, multiply its length by its width.

5 cm × 3 cm = 15 cm^2

The area of this shape is 15 cm^2.

To find the area of an irregular shape, you may have to split it up into smaller squares or rectangles. Or you may have to count squares on a grid. Count the whole squares within the shape followed by those squares where half or more than half of the square is included in the shape. The total is an approximate estimate of the shape's area.

"I get perimeter and area muddled."

Think of a **hedge** going round the **edge** of a really muddy field!

The hedge makes the **perimeter** and is 'so many' metres **long**. The field it encloses has an **area** of 'so many' metres **square**.

Look at this example:

> **What are the width and area of a rectangular field if the perimeter is 260 m and the length of the field is 90 m?**
>
> perimeter = 2 × length + 2 × width
>
> 260 m = 2 × 90 m + 2*w*
>
> 260 m = 180 m + 2*w*
>
> 260 m − 180 m = 2*w*
>
> 80 m = 2*w*
>
> 40 m = *w*
>
> Width = **40 m**
>
> **Area:** length × width = 90 m × 40 m = **3600 m²**
>
> 90 m
>
> 90 m

We can use the same formula to find the area of a parallelogram: base × height.

But be sure to remember to use the **height** of the parallelogram, not the length of one of the other sides.

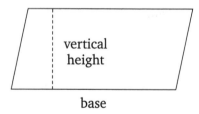

vertical height

base

(To find the area of a triangle, see page 53.)

Key facts

- The **perimeter** of a 2D shape is the total distance round the **edge** of the shape and can be measured in mm, cm, m or km.

- The **area** of a 2D shape is the space **inside** the perimeter, which could be coloured in. It can be measured in cm², m² or km².

- To calculate the perimeter or area of a shape you need to know the distance along each side of the shape.

㉑ *3D shapes*

Naming 3D shapes

You need to recognise and be able to name these 3D shapes:

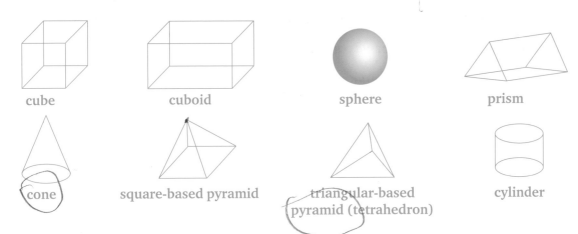

cube   cuboid   sphere   prism

cone   square-based pyramid   triangular-based pyramid (tetrahedron)   cylinder

Prisms have the same shape at both ends with rectangles or squares joining the two ends together. Prisms are named according to their end shape:

triangular prism   **pentagonal prism**   **hexagonal prism**

Nets

A net is the shape you would draw, cut out and fold to make a 3D shape. To work out from a diagram whether a net will make a shape, you have to imagine cutting it out and folding it into the shape.

There are many ways of making the net of a cube. Here are two ways:

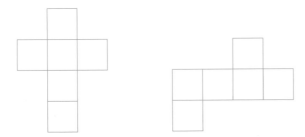

Faces, edges and vertices

The faces of a solid 3D shape are the flat parts.

The **edges** of a solid 3D shape are where two faces meet.

The vertices of a solid 3D shape are the points or corners.

Look back at the diagrams of the 3D shapes on page 59.

How many faces does a square-based pyramid have?

How many edges does a cuboid have?

How many vertices does a sphere have?

> **REMEMBER!**
>
> The plural of vertex is **vertices**.
> A cone has one vertex.
> A cube has eight vertices.

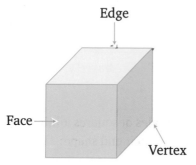

Edge

Face

Vertex

Key facts

- **Prisms** have the same shape at both ends with rectangles or squares joining the two ends together.
- A **net** is the shape you would draw, cut out and fold to make a 3D shape.
- The **faces** of a solid 3D shape are the flat parts.
- The **edges** of a solid 3D shape are where two faces meet.
- The **vertices** of a solid 3D shape are the points or corners.

22) *Volume and capacity*

Volume

The volume of a solid 3D object is the amount of space it takes up. To find the volume of a cube or cuboid, multiply together the three dimensions: length, breadth and height.

Volume of a cuboid = $l \times b \times h$

> **REMEMBER!**
>
> Volume is measured in **cubic centimetres** (cm^3) or cubic metres (m^3)

The dimensions of this cuboid are:

$l = 4$ cm

$b = 3$ cm

$h = 2$ cm

The volume of the cuboid is $4 \times 3 \times 2 = 24$ cm^3

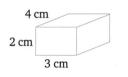

To find the volume of an irregular solid object, split it up into smaller cubes or cuboids and find their separate volumes. Then add up the volumes.

Look at this irregular solid object. It can be split into two separate cuboids:

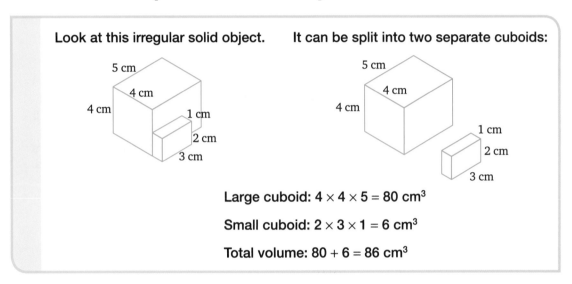

Large cuboid: $4 \times 4 \times 5 = 80$ cm^3

Small cuboid: $2 \times 3 \times 1 = 6$ cm^3

Total volume: $80 + 6 = 86$ cm^3

Capacity

The capacity of a container is how much water or other liquid it will hold. Capacity can be measured in **litres** (l) and/or **millilitres** (ml).

For example:
the amount 900 ml can also be written as 0.9 litre
the amount 1400 ml can also be written as 1 l 400 ml or 1.4 l.

One litre is just under two pints and is the amount in a standard carton of juice; it will give you four large glasses of juice.

A teacup holds about 200 ml.

A mug holds about 300 ml.

REMEMBER!

1 litre = 1000 millilitres

Key facts

- Volume is the amount of space an object takes up and is measured in **cubic centimetres (cm³)** or **cubic metres (m³)**.

- Volume of a cube/cuboid = **length** × **breadth** × **height** ($l \times b \times h$).

- Capacity is the amount of liquid a container will hold and is measured in **litres (l)** and/or **millilitres (ml)**.

(23) *Coordinates and transformations*

Coordinates

In questions about transformations, the corners (or vertices) of shapes are given as coordinates, such as **(3, 2)**. You may have to plot the shape on the **x-** and **y-axes** yourself.

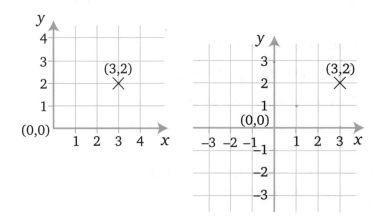

REMEMBER!

Try remembering that you go **'along the hall** first (*x*-axis), and then **up or down the stairs** (*y*-axis)' when giving a pair of coordinates.

The first number in a pair of coordinates is always the x amount, the distance you have to go **along** the **x-axis**.

The second number in a pair of coordinates is always the y amount, the distance you have to go **up or down** the **y-axis**.

Reflection, rotation and translation

There are three main types of **transformation:** reflection, rotation **and** translation.

Reflection means the result of reflecting a shape in a given mirror line.

Rotation means swivelling a shape round a given point or centre of rotation. An object can be rotated **clockwise**, like the hands of a clock, or anticlockwise, the opposite way from the hands of a clock.

clockwise   anticlockwise

Translation means moving a shape along and up or down.

Look at this example:

1 Plot these coordinates on the grid.
    (–2, 2), (–2, 4), (–5, 2)
    Join them together (shape A).

2 Reflect the shape along the line *y* = 1 (shape B).

3 Rotate the original shape 180° clockwise about the point (0, 0) (shape C).

4 Translate shape C 1 square left and 4 squares down (shape D).

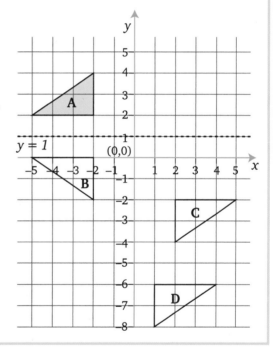

Key facts

- **Coordinates** tell you a specific point on a grid.
- The value on the *x*-axis is always given **before** the value on the *y*-axis: (*x*, *y*).
- **Reflection** is the result of reflecting a shape in a mirror line.
- **Rotation** means turning a shape round a point or centre of rotation.
- **Clockwise** is in the same direction as the hands of a clock, **anticlockwise** is the opposite direction to the hands of a clock.
- **Translation** means moving a shape along and/or up or down.

(24) *Symmetry*

Line symmetry

A shape is said to have line symmetry (or be symmetric) when it can be divided into two identical, mirror images by a **line of symmetry**. Shapes can have more than one line of symmetry. Lines of symmetry are usually shown as dotted lines on a diagram:

Sometimes a line of symmetry is shown next to a shape and not on it at all. The shape is reflected symmetrically as if the line is a mirror. The distances between the points or vertices of the shape from the line of symmetry must be the same for both the shape and its reflected image:

> **REMEMBER!**
>
> Folding is a good way to check if a line is a line of symmetry. The two sides must map onto each other exactly.

Rotational symmetry

A shape has rotational symmetry if you can turn it around its centre and it maps (or fits) exactly on top of, itself.

The number of times it does this is its order of rotational symmetry.

This star has rotational order of rotational symmetry 5 because it maps onto itself 5 times before arriving back at where it started.

Key facts

- A shape is said to be **symmetric** when it can be split into two identical, mirror images by a **line of symmetry**.
- Shapes can have more than one line of symmetry.
- A shape is described as having **rotational symmetry** if, when you turn it round, it maps onto itself exactly.
- The number of times a shape maps onto itself is its **order of rotational symmetry**.

Exam tips

In an exam, remember that you can rotate your page if you need to. You can also sketch out a quick diagram if it helps you. For symmetry questions, work point-to-point from wherever the mirror line is, whether the mirror line is vertical, horizontal or diagonal.

Measurement

(25) *Metric and imperial units of measurement*

Metric measurements

> **REMEMBER!**
>
> milli → 1000th   centi → 100th   deci → 10th   kilo → 1000

> **REMEMBER!**
>
> ≈ means 'approximately equal to'.

All metric units of measurement use tens, hundreds and thousands and are simpler to use than imperial units. Here are some details of metric units used to measure length, mass and capacity:

Metric equivalents	Examples
Length:	
1 km (kilometre) = **1000 m** (metres)	Kilometres are used to measure large distances between villages, towns and cities.
1 m = 100 cm (centimetres)	**1 m** is the length of a **metre stick** (look for one at school!).
1 cm = 10 mm (millimetres)	**1 cm** is about the width of your **fingertip**. **1 mm** is the width of a large **full stop**.

Metric equivalents	Examples
Mass	
1 t (tonne) = **1000 kg** (kilograms)	**1 tonne** is about the weight of a **small car**.
1 kg = 1000 g (grams)	**1 kg** is the weight of a **bag of sugar**. 1 kg ≈ 2.2 lb
1 g = 1000 mg (milligrams)	**1 g** is the weight of a **paper clip**. Ingredients in medicines are often measured in milligrams.

Metric equivalents	Examples	
Capacity		
1 l (litre) = **1000 ml** (millilitres)	**1 l** is the capacity of a standard **fruit juice carton**.	
	500 ml is the capacity of a standard **washing-up liquid bottle**.	
	330 ml is the capacity of a standard **drink can**.	
	5 ml is the capacity of a **teaspoon**.	

Imperial measurements

Imperial units of measurement were used before metric ones replaced them. Imperial measurements continue to be used, particularly on road signs giving distances in miles. It is therefore important for you to know them and their equivalent metric amounts.

Imperial measurement	Approximate metric equivalents
Length	
1 mile = 1760 yards	Almost 2 km. 8 km ≈ 5 miles
1 yard (yd) = 3 feet	Just under 1 metre.
1 foot (ft) = 12 inches	The length of a 30 cm ruler. The height of a tall man is about 6 ft or just under 2 m. 1 inch ≈ 2.5 cm

Imperial measurement	Approximate metric equivalents	
Mass		
1 stone = 14 pounds	Just over 6 kg.	
1 pound (lb) = 16 ounces (oz)	The amount of honey in a jar – almost 500 g.	
1 ounce (oz)	The weight of three £1 coins. $1 \text{ oz} \approx 30 \text{ g}$	

Imperial measurement	Approximate metric equivalents	
Capacity		
1 gallon = 8 pints	$1 \text{ gallon} \approx 4\,l$	
1 pint	$1 \text{ pint} \approx \frac{1}{2}$ litre Milk is sometimes sold in pints.	

It is important for you to know what these metric and imperial measurements look or feel like.

Exam tips

In an exam, make sure that you know the conversions: for example, the number of millilitres in a litre, grams in a kilogram or metres in a kilometre. It is also helpful to have a picture in your mind of examples of the different measurements. For example, a can of pop is 330 ml and the height of an average door is just under 2 m.

Measurement

Imperial measurement	Approximate metric equivalents	
Mass		
1 stone = 14 pounds	Just over 6 kg.	
1 pound (lb) = 16 ounces (oz)	The amount of honey in a jar – almost 500 g.	
1 ounce (oz)	The weight of three £1 coins. $1 \text{ oz} \approx 30 \text{ g}$	

Imperial measurement	Approximate metric equivalents	
Capacity		
1 gallon = 8 pints	$1 \text{ gallon} \approx 4\,l$	
1 pint	$1 \text{ pint} \approx \frac{1}{2}$ litre Milk is sometimes sold in pints.	

It is important for you to know what these metric and imperial measurements look or feel like.

Exam tips

In an exam, make sure that you know the conversions: for example, the number of millilitres in a litre, grams in a kilogram or metres in a kilometre. It is also helpful to have a picture in your mind of examples of the different measurements. For example, a can of pop is 330 ml and the height of an average door is just under 2 m.

Key facts

- There are **metric** and **imperial** units of measurement.

- Metric units of measurement are all based on **tens, hundreds** and **thousands**:

  1 km = 1000 m
  1 m = 100 cm
  1 cm = 10 mm
  1 tonne = 1000 kg
  1 kg = 1000 g
  1 g = 1000 mg
  1 litre = 1000 ml

- Imperial units of measurement include **miles, stones** and **pints**:

  1 mile = 1760 yards
  1 yard (yd) = 3 feet
  1 foot (ft) = 12 inches
  1 stone = 14 pounds
  1 pound (lb) = 16 ounces (oz)
  1 gallon = 8 pints

- These **approximate equivalences** show the relationships between metric and imperial measures:

  1 mile ≈ 2 km
  1 yard ≈ 1 metre
  1 kg ≈ 2.2 lb
  1 ounce (oz) ≈ 30 grams (g) or 0.03 kilograms (kg)
  1 pint ≈ $\frac{1}{2}$ litre (l) or 500 millilitres (ml) or 0.500 l

㉖ *Reading scales*

Types of scales

A scale can be read in a straight line like a ruler or round like a dial.

It is very important to look carefully for the unit of measurement given on a scale.

The jug says 1 litre at the top. The markings below it represent 50 millilitres and 100 millilitres.

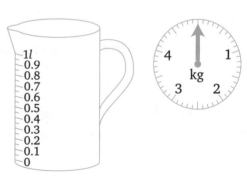

The round dial says kg, meaning kilograms; therefore the smaller divisions each represent 100 grams.

It is important to work out what one division on a scale is measuring.

> **REMEMBER!**
>
> 1 l = 1000 ml
> 850 ml = 0.850 l
> 1 kg = 1000 g
> 28 g = 0.028 kg

Here are some 1-litre jugs, each with different division lines marked on them:

A 1000 ml ÷ 4 equal size sections = 250 ml per section.
So jug A contains 250 ml + 250 ml + $\frac{1}{2}$ of 250 ml = 625 ml.

B 1000 ml ÷ 5 equal size sections = 200 ml per section.
So jug B contains 2 × 200 ml = 400 ml.

C 1000 ml ÷ 10 equal size sections = 100 ml per section.
So jug C contains 9 × 100 ml = 900 ml.

D 1000 ml ÷ 20 equal size sections = 50 ml per section.
So jug D contains 1000 − (3 × 50 ml) = 850 ml.

You also need to be able to measure angles by reading the scale on a protractor.

- Line up the bottom line of the angle with the base line of the protractor. Make sure the point of the angle is at the centre of the cross in the middle of the protractor.
- Find the scale that starts at 0 degrees for your angle. In the example below you want the inner scale.
- Read off the size of the angle using the correct scale. This angle is 45°.

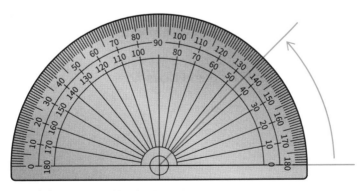

(27) *Time and timetables*

Telling the time

Telling the time is an essential skill. You need to be able to tell the time in words using a clock with hands (analogue time) and write a time in figures (digital time).

The 12-hour clock is based on the day having two sets of 12 hours. To make the difference clear between the times, **a.m.** (morning) or **p.m.** (afternoon) is written after the time. So, 9.00 a.m. is 9 o'clock in the morning and 9.00 p.m. is 9 o'clock in the evening.

The 24-hour clock is shown on some digital clocks. It continues after 12.00 at lunchtime like this: 13.00, 14.00, and so on, with 13.00 being 1 o'clock and 14.00 being 2 o'clock. So, 16.00 is 4 o'clock in the afternoon.

24-hour clock times always have four digits and therefore have a '0' written before the hours 1 to 9 in the morning: 03.25.

9:00

9 o'clock

REMEMBER!

Midnight in the 24-hour clock is zero hours: 00.00.

Months

It is important to know how many days are in each month of the year.

This poem can help you to remember how long each month lasts:

30 days have September, April, June and November
All the rest have 31
Excepting February alone
Which has 28 days clear
And 29 in each leap year.

REMEMBER!

In this book, whenever a new maths word is introduced, it is printed in red. If you need to, you can check its meaning in the Glossary at the back of the book.

Timetables

Timetables generally use the 24-hour clock.

To find the difference between two times, it can be useful to count the whole hours first and then count the minutes.

Look at this example:

> If a bus leaves at 09.16 and arrives at its destination at 16.03,
> how long did the 09.16 → 15.16 = 6 hours
>   15.16 → 16.03 = 47 minutes
>
> The journey took 6 hours 47 minutes.

Key facts

- The **12-hour clock** uses the hours 1 to 12 twice in one day. Use **a.m.** to show a time in the morning and **p.m.** to show a time in the afternoon or evening.

- The **24-hour clock** uses the hours 00.00 to 24.00, with 00.00 being midnight and 12.00 being midday. You do not use a.m. and p.m. with 24-hour times.

- Know how many days there are in each month, and the order of the months of the year.

- **Timetables** generally use the 24-hour clock.

Everyday practice

There are so many things that you can do to help your child with the 11+ exam. Building their knowledge through experiences and opportunities is far better than sitting and learning lists. Some of these activities underpin 11+ knowledge and concepts while other activities help to provide a more holistic education. Hopefully there are some ideas here that your child will enjoy:

Games and activities

Board or pieces games

There are many games that extend skills in numeracy, data, shape, space, strategic thinking, logic and problem solving, and do so in the most fun way:

> Cluedo™, Monopoly™, Yahtzee™, Skyjo™, Countdown™, Brainbox Maths™, Nimnik Tumbling Towers™, Azul™, Rummikub™, Villanious™, Kerplunk™, Qwirkle™, Sagrada™, IQ Games™, Chess, Draughts, Battleships and Backgammon as well as card games and jigsaws

Console, computer, phone games

These games are portable, played by just one child and can both extend and consolidate maths skills. There are many games and apps that cover times tables and number bonds, but games that develop more problem-solving skills include:

> The Sims, Sim City, Tetris, Lego World, City Skylines, Buzz Brain and Big Brain Academy

Strategic games such as FIFA that require virtual 'football team manager' skills are excellent at working to a budget, controlling costs, positioning players and so on. All are important maths skills.

Car games

Although many children might play paper games or online games when they are travelling, there are some other great opportunities for fun learning on the road:

- What Number Am I? – think of a number for your child to work out. You could say things like, "When I double it and subtract 7, my answer is 19. What number am I?" This can be made as easy or as difficult as you want.

- Sequences – the first person begins with the number 1. The second person gives another number to create the first two terms of a sequence, the next person must come up with a third number that continues a sequence and this continues until someone makes a mistake. This could be as simple as +2 each time or could be far more complex, such as ×4 then halve, or +2, +4, +8, etc.

- Doggies and Moggies – give your child a number and they have to find a way of reaching it by only dividing or multiplying. If you said '36' correct answers could include 72 ÷ 2, 144 ÷ 4, 2 × 18, 3 × 12, 4 × 9, 6 × 6 but don't allow 36 × 1! You can adapt the difficulty of the number or you could ask specifically for a 'doggy' (division) or a 'moggy' (multiplication).

Active games

Many traditional street games include strategies for problem solving, consolidating numbers and working with angles and shapes. Throwing a ball against the wall and jumping over it as it lands, playing hopscotch and even hide and seek are all relevant.

If you have a sandpit or paddling pool and you can include measuring, sandcastle building, creating a water course through dams and bridges or any other hands-on activities it can consolidate measurement and problem solving, especially if you give a specific task.

For example, the task could be to create a bridge from paper, over some water, that can hold the weight of a toy car. Another task might be to create a sand structure that reaches 50 cm in height.

You could also play 'kitchen hunt' or 'bathroom hunt': ask your child to find 10 different items with different measurements marked on them, focusing on grams and kilograms in the kitchen or millilitres and litres in the bathroom. This helps children develop mind-pictures of what different things weigh or measure.

Another practical task is to spot right-angles around the house using a piece of paper folded once and then again along the fold to make a right-angle tester. Children love doing this and it is really interesting for them to see how doors, windows, shelves, tables and so on have lots of right angles but chairs or sofas have far fewer, and to discuss why that might be.

Days out

There is a wealth of places to visit that help children to interact with the world, to extend their mathematical knowledge and to develop their ability to learn. Many big attractions such as museums, castles, stately homes, National Trust properties, zoos and festivals have activity packs for children and some offer guided tours geared to children, especially during holiday times.

Science museums, planetariums, natural history events and steam fairs are all valuable for underpinning mathematical concepts.

Technology centres, steam fairs, transport museums and working industrial museums can spark an interest in Science and Technology and their mathematical concepts. Planning and riding on a car journey is the perfect way to investigate speed, distance and time – and map reading.

Taking a bus or train journey provides the opportunity for reading maps and checking timetables.

Other hands-on activities

These are games or activities that one child can do by themselves and strengthen skills in accurate number work, strategic thinking, problem solving and shape/space awareness. Examples include:

- Sudoku or other number-based puzzles.
- Construction games such as Lego, K'nex, Meccano or Airfix models that have a diagram with a step-by-step guide for children to follow or for them to create their own original constructs.
- Jigsaw puzzles – the number of pieces and the subject matter can be varied to suit the ability of the child.
- Model making; following patterns through knitting, sewing, knotting, weaving etc.
- Learning a musical instrument and reading music.
- Cooking, using a recipe, including baking and smoothie-making.
- Activities that require balance, repetition of action for accuracy, problem solving or working to a rhythm are also good; for example, martial arts, sports and dance.
- Orienteering is brilliant for map reading skills.
- Origami is a great way of practising all kinds of geometry skills, as well as improving dexterity and coordination.

Top ten everyday activities

1   Encourage your child to use his or her skills in everyday situations. For example, when you're shopping, ask your child to work out the cost of a few items or to say how much change you will receive.

2   Use every opportunity to show your child practical ways of applying their multiplication and division skills. For example, when calculating the total cost of several of the same item or when sharing out pocket money.

3   Encourage your child to look out for types of numbers so he or she can become familiar with them. For instance, Roman numerals are often seen on clock faces; negative numbers on thermometers or weather forecasts.

4   Help your child to see patterns wherever possible, for example in tiles and fabrics or in flowers and plants, and to relate them to number.

5   Visiting shops or shopping online during the sales will give lots of opportunities to help your child work out new prices by calculating and subtracting the percentage discounts.

6   Using props such as tangerine segments, chocolate chunks, coins, sweets and so on, try to work out ratio, proportion and fractions. This can help your child to visualise the amounts involved.

7   Helping with cooking and baking are practical activities that can help with visualising capacities. Comparing the capacity of a range of bathroom or kitchen container or bottles will strengthen your child's understanding.

8   Ask your child to use a timetable to work out how long a journey will be. Ask them to work out how many days it will be until a certain date or to work out what day the 17th will fall on. Ask them to work out how long it will be until bedtime or what the time was 12 hours previously. All of these tasks will really help to consolidate time skills.

9   Teach your child how to wrap presents effectively so that they have hands-on experience of surface area.

10   Open a savings account for your child and encourage them to see how much interest their money is earning and discuss how long it might take for their money to grow to certain amounts. It is a good opportunity for them to round money up or down and to plan ahead.

Glossary

24-hour clock – the 24-hour clock uses the hours 00.00 to 24.00, with 00.00 being midnight and 12.00 being midday.

acute angle – an angle of less than 90°.

acute-angled triangle – this has three acute angles.

algebra – the part of maths that deals with finding unknown numbers in equations.

a.m. – the time between midnight and midday.

analogue time – the time written or described in words using a clock with hands.

angle – measured in degrees, an angle tells us how far something turns or rotates.

anticlockwise – describing movement in the opposite direction to the way the hands of a clock move.

arc – a part of the circumference of a circle.

area – how much space there is inside a 2D shape, measured in square units, for example, cm², m², km².

average – a typical value of a set of data.

axis (plural: axes) – a graph has two lines called axes, the x-axis and y-axis, which join or intersect at the origin.

bearing – an angle between the direction north and the direction in which something is travelling.

cancelling – using division to find an equivalent fraction in its lowest terms.

capacity – how much liquid a container will hold, measured in litres (l) or millilitres (ml), or pints or gallons.

circumference – the distance around the edge of a circle.

clockwise – describing movement in the same direction as the hands of a clock.

common denominator – when comparing, adding or subtracting fractions, the fractions need to be changed to equivalent fractions with the same denominator: this is called a common denominator and will be the lowest common multiple of the original denominators.

common fraction – the numerator and denominator in a common fraction are both whole numbers.

concentric circles – circles that share the same centre point but have a different radius.

cone – a 3D shape which has one flat face in the shape of a circle. The body of the shape is curved and leads up to a point or vertex (like an ice cream cone).

consecutive numbers – numbers that follow on in order.

coordinates – these indicate the position of a point on a graph, for example, (3, 4). The first number is the distance you move in the x-direction; the second number is the distance you move in the y-direction.

cube – a 3D shape with six identical square faces.

cube number – a number that is multiplied by itself twice.

cuboid – a 3D shape which has six rectangular faces.

cylinder – a 3D shape with a circle at each end and a curved surface joining them (like a tube or pipe).

data – collections of information.

decagon – a polygon with ten sides.

decimal fraction – tenths, hundredths, thousandths, etc. shown as digits after a decimal point.

decimal number – a number written with a decimal point.

degrees – angles are measured in degrees. A small circle at the top right-hand side of the number is written to show that the measurement is in degrees. There are 360° in a full turn.

denominator – the bottom part of a fraction; it tells you how many equal parts the amount has been divided into.

diagonal – slanting. A diagonal joins two vertices of a polygon. A rectangle has two diagonals.

diameter – the distance straight across a circle from circumference to circumference, going through the centre.

digit – a single number from 0 to 9.

digital time – the time written in numbers, as you would see on a digital clock.

divisible – a number is divisible by a smaller number if the smaller number divides exactly into the larger number.

edge – the line where two faces of a solid 3D shape meet.

equation – a number sentence with an equals sign (=). The left-hand side has the same value as the right-hand side.

equilateral triangle – this has three equal sides and three equal angles.

equivalent fractions – fractions that are equal to one another.

estimate – make a sensible guess at an answer.

face – one surface of a solid 3D shape.

factor – a whole number that will divide exactly into another number.

fraction – a part of something.

graph – a visual way of displaying data; it can have bars, lines or pictures representing the data.

heptagon – a polygon with seven sides.

hexagon – a polygon with six sides.

highest common factor (HCF) – the HCF of a set of numbers is the largest number that is a factor of all numbers in the set.

horizontal – straight across.

hundredth – one divided into 100 equal parts gives one hundred hundredths.

improper fraction – a top-heavy fraction where the numerator is larger than the denominator.

index (plural: indices) – the number of times a number is multiplied by itself. For example, $2 \times 2 \times 2 = 2^3$ has an index of 3.

integer – a whole number.

inverse – the opposite of something.

inverse operations – using the opposite of add, subtract, multiply or divide to find missing numbers.

irregular polygon – a 2D shape with sides that are not all the same length and the angles might not be the same.

isosceles triangle – this has two equal sides and two equal angles.

kite – a 2D shape with two pairs of equal-length sides that are adjacent, or next to each other. It has one pair of opposite equal angles and one line of symmetry.

line symmetry – a shape has line symmetry when it can be divided into two identical, mirror images. We say it is symmetric.

lowest common multiple (LCM) – the LCM of a set of numbers is the smallest number that is a multiple of all numbers in the set.

lowest terms – a common fraction written using the smallest numbers possible.

mean – the number or value found by adding together all of the numbers in a set and dividing by how many numbers there are in the set.

median – the middle number or value in a set when the numbers are put in order of size.

mixed number – a mixture of a whole number and a fraction.

mode – the number or value in a set of data that occurs most often.

multiple – a multiple of a number is the answer when the number is multiplied by another number.

negative number – a number that is less than zero.

net – the shape you would draw, cut out and fold to make a 3D shape.

nonagon – a polygon with nine sides.

numerator – the top part of a fraction; it tells you how many equal parts you are interested in.

obtuse angle – an angle greater than 90° but less than 180°.

obtuse-angled triangle – this has one obtuse angle.

octagon – a polygon with eight sides.

order of rotational symmetry – the number of times a shape maps exactly onto itself when turned around its centre.

origin – the point (0, 0) on a graph.

parallel – lines that are parallel never meet but run the same distance apart from each other for their entire length; they are not necessarily straight or equal in length.

parallelogram – a 2D shape with two pairs of parallel sides, two equal acute angles and two equal obtuse angles. It has no lines of symmetry.

pentagon – a polygon with five sides.

percentage – out of 100.

perimeter – the total distance around the edge of a 2D shape.

perpendicular – two lines are perpendicular if they are at right angles to each other.

pie chart – a circle divided into sections to show the proportions of how something is shared into groups.

p.m. – the time between midday and midnight.

polygon – a 2D shape with three or more straight sides.

positive number – a number that is more than zero.

prime factor – the prime factors of a number are the prime numbers which can be multiplied together to make that number.

prime number – a prime number has only two factors: 1 and the number itself.

prism – a 3D shape with the same shape at each end and rectangles or squares joining the two ends together.

probability – the chance or possibility of something happening, usually written as a fraction.

proportion – the fraction of the total amount when you divide up that amount using a given ratio.

quadrilateral – a four-sided, 2D shape.

quotient – the number you get when you divide one number by another.

radius (plural: radii) – the distance from the centre of a circle to the circumference; half the diameter.

range – the range of a set of numbers or values is the difference between the smallest number and the largest number.

ratio – a ratio is used to compare two or more numbers or quantities and is usually expressed with a colon between the numbers.

rectangle – a 2D shape with two pairs of parallel sides of equal length, four right angles and two lines of symmetry.

reflection – the result of reflecting a shape in a given mirror line.

reflex angle – an angle greater than 180° and less than 360°.

regular polygon – a 2D shape with sides the same length and with all angles equal.

remainder – the amount left over when one number doesn't divide exactly into another.

rhombus – a 2D shape with four equal sides, two equal acute angles, two equal obtuse angles and two lines of symmetry.

right angle – an angle of 90° (think of the corner of a piece of paper).

right-angled triangle – this has one right angle.

Roman numerals – capital letters, once used by Romans, which represent numbers.

rotation – turning a shape around a given point or centre of rotation, either clockwise or anticlockwise.

rotational symmetry – a shape has rotational symmetry if when you turn it around its centre it maps onto, or fits exactly on top of, itself.

scalene triangle – this has no equal sides and no equal angles.

semicircle – half a circle.

sector – part of a circle, between two radii and an arc.

simplest terms – see lowest terms.

sphere – a 3D version of a circle: a ball.

square – a 2D shape with four equal sides, four right angles and four lines of symmetry.

square-based pyramid – a 3D shape with a square base whose other edges meet at a point.

square number – the result of multiplying a number by itself.

square root – the square root of a number is the number you multiply by itself to make that number.

symmetric – see line symmetry.

tenth – one divided into 10 equal parts give ten tenths.

tetrahedron – see triangular-based pyramid.

thousandth – one divided into 1000 equal parts give a thousand thousandths.

transformation – changing a shape through reflection, rotation or translation.

translation – moving a shape right or left, and/or up or down.

trapezium – a 2D shape that looks like a triangle with its head chopped off! Two of its sides are parallel.

triangular-based pyramid – a 3D shape with a triangular base whose other edges meet at a point.

triangular number – a number that can be arranged as a triangle using, for example, dots.

units of measurement – different ways of measuring money, time, length, mass, capacity, distance or volume and so on. Units of measurement are either metric, based on multiples of ten, or imperial, based on historic ways of measuring.

value – how much something is worth.

Venn diagram – a diagram in which data is organised into overlapping rings.

vertex (plural: vertices) – the point or corner made by two intersecting straight lines or by the edges of a solid 3D shape.

vertical – straight up or down.

volume – the amount of space a solid 3D object takes up, measured in cm^3 or m^3.

whole number – a number that does not have any fraction part to it. The counting numbers are whole numbers.

x-axis – the horizontal line on a graph that joins or intersects the y-axis at the origin.

y-axis – the vertical line on a graph that joins or intersects the x-axis at the origin.

OXFORD
UNIVERSITY PRESS

Great Clarendon Street, Oxford, OX2 6DP, United Kingdom

Oxford University Press is a department of the University of Oxford.
It furthers the University's objective of excellence in research, scholarship,
and education by publishing worldwide. Oxford is a registered trade mark
of Oxford University Press in the UK and in certain other countries

British Library Cataloguing in Publication Data
Data available

ISBN: 978-0-19-277616-7

10 9 8 7 6 5 4 3

Paper used in the production of this book is a natural, recyclable product
made from wood grown in sustainable forests. The manufacturing process
conforms to the environmental regulations of the country of origin.

Printed in Poland by Opolgraf SA

Acknowledgements

The Publishers would like to thank Michellejoy Hughes for her contribution
to this edition.

Cover illustrations by Lo Cole